Miracles & the new psychology; a study in the healing miracles of the New Testament

Edward Romilly Micklem M.A.

BIBLIOLIFE

MIRACLES & THE NEW PSYCHOLOGY

A Study in the

Healing Miracles of the New Testament

BY

E. R. MICKLEM

M.A., B LITT. (OXON)

OXFORD UNIVERSITY PRESS

LONDON: HUMPHREY MILFORD

1922

PREFACE

At a day when no Englishman would boggle at construing 'je vais de mieux en mieux', and when every man suspects his neighbour of an 'Oedipus complex' some apology seems needed for yet another volume with 'psychology' on the title-page. My excuse is the very prevalence of this word on the lips of the community. According to many, psychology will 'explain' everything however mysterious or however sacred. Human affection and love is nothing but a manifestation of the primitive sex instinct, prayer is 'merely autosuggestion', effective intercession 'just telepathy', while religion is a sure sign of 'infantile regression'. Sweeping assertions are, as a rule, misleading, and are especially unfortunate when they bring discredit on a method of great value. The only useful reply to them is a dispassionate examination of the ascertainable facts. In the following pages I have attempted such an examination of a subject which has suffered much from broad generalizations.

It is impossible to acknowledge by name all those who have given me valuable assistance in the preparation of this study. Some few, however, who have gone out of their way to give me help and advice I cannot refrain from naming: Dr. W. B. Selbie, Dr. G. Buchanan Gray, Dr. William Brown, Dr. J. A. Hadfield, the Rev. Canon B. H. Streeter, the Rev. Gordon Matthews, Dr. E. J. Peill, my brother Dr. T. E. Micklem, and, above all, my brother the Rev. N. Micklem, without whose unstinted help and continual counsel and encouragement the book would not have been written. For the views propounded none but myself is responsible.

If there is anything here that contributes to sound learning and true religion I dedicate it to my Father and my Mother.

E. ROMILLY MICKLEM.

Mansfield College,
May, 1922.

CONTENTS

		PAGES
	PREFACE	2
I.	GENERAL INTRODUCTION	5-6
II.	BRIEF INTRODUCTION TO PSYCHOTHERAPY .	6-22
III.	INTRODUCTION TO SOURCES	
	A. Synoptic Gospels	23-25
	B. Fourth Gospel	25-28
	C. Acts	28-30
IV	BELIEFS CURRENT IN N. T. TIMES LIABLE TO AFFECT DIAGNOSIS OF DISEASE AND METHODS OF HEALING:	
	A. Relation between Sin and Suffering . .	31-34
	B. Belief in Demons	34-42
V.	LEPROSY	
	Introduction—Critical Examination of Cases—Cases viewed in the Light of Psychotherapy . . .	43-50
VI.	DEMON POSSESSION	
	A. Introduction—Critical Examination of Cases .	50-61
	B. Demon Possession in the Mission-field . . .	61-71
	C. Demon Possession viewed in the Light of Morbid Psychology and of Psychotherapy . . .	71-80
VII.	FEVER	
	Critical Examination of Cases—Cases viewed in the Light of Psychotherapy	81-84
VIII.	PARALYSIS	
	Critical Examination of Cases, &c.	85-98
IX.	LAMENESS	
	Critical Examination of Cases, &c. . . .	99-101
X.	BLINDNESS	
	Critical Examination of Cases, &c. . . .	101-114

		PAGES
XI.	'DEAF STAMMERER'	114-120
XII.	WOMAN WITH A HAEMORRHAGE.	120-123
XIII.	WOMAN WITH A 'SPIRIT OF INFIRMITY' . .	124-125
XIV.	DROPSY.	125-126
XV.	RESTORATION OF EAR OF HIGH PRIEST'S SERVANT	127-128
XVI.	RAISINGS FROM THE DEAD	128-129
XVII.	GENERAL SUMMARY AND CONCLUSION . . .	130-136
	INDEX OF NAMES	137
	INDEX OF BIBLICAL REFERENCES	140

LIST OF ABBREVIATIONS EMPLOYED

B. Chr. — Foakes Jackson and Lake, *The Beginnings of Christianity.*

E. B. — *Encyclopaedia Biblica.*

E. R. E. — Hastings's *Encyclopaedia of Religion and Ethics.*

E. S. — Loisy, *Les Évangiles synoptiques.*

G. H. T. — Burkitt, *The Gospel History and its Transmission.*

I. L. N T. — Moffatt, *Introduction to the Literature of the New Testament*, 3rd edition.

J. E. — *Jewish Encyclopaedia.*

Jn. — Author of the Fourth Gospel.

J. Q. R. — *Jewish Quarterly Review.*

Lk. — Author of the Third Gospel ; author of Acts.

Mk. — Author of the Second Gospel.

M. N. T. — J. M. Thompson, *Miracles in the New Testament.*

Mt. — Author of the First Gospel.

O. S. S. P. — *Oxford Studies in the Synoptic Problem.*

P. C. — Peake's *Commentary on the Bible.*

S. G. — Montefiore, *The Synoptic Gospels.*

S. H. N. S. — *Seale Hayne Neurological Studies.*

1

GENERAL INTRODUCTION

In this essay the expression 'miracles of healing in the New Testament' is employed in its popular sense as covering all those cases of works of healing done by our Lord or His followers that are recorded in the New Testament. A discussion of such a question as the possibility or impossibility of 'miracle' in a more restricted and technical sense (whatever may be the precise definition attached to the term) is not relevant to the study undertaken. Nor, when the healing acts of our Lord are under consideration, is it necessary, or even desirable, to express any particular metaphysical theory as to the nature of His Person. On the other hand it would be a travesty of an investigation into His healing ministry from a psychological standpoint if His personality were to be ignored. It would be universally acknowledged by those competent to judge that the success of any modern doctor, whether or not he be a specialist in psychotherapy, depends to a very considerable extent upon his own personality; and it is reasonable to suppose that this factor played a prominent part in the cures of Jesus Christ. I take as postulates, without attempting any detailed proof, that Jesus manifested a remarkably keen insight into human character, and that He gave the impression of a man of real sympathy and authority. These traits, which have an important bearing on the present study, seem to me to stand out unquestionably in the Gospel narratives.

The order which I have adopted will be apparent from the preceding Table of Contents. It should, perhaps, be said with regard to Section II (Introduction to Psychotherapy) that much in it that may seem at first sight to be somewhat remote from the subject of the N. T. miracles will appear to be relevant as the essay progresses.

In attempting to adduce parallels to the cases under consideration I have confined myself almost exclusively to evidence from medical practitioners in psychotherapy whose practice is not officially connected with healing of a specifically religious kind. Hence I have not quoted any examples from Lourdes, the work of Christian Scientists, that of the Emmanuel Movement in America, or the like, although I do not wish to deny that striking cures have been performed in such places and movements. On the other hand, I have thought it desirable to cite evidence from the Christian mission-field in order to illustrate my argument when dealing with 'demon possession'. The departure which I have made from my rule about evidence from religious healing in the case of the man with the 'withered hand' does not, I think, need special justification.

In a few instances I have added in a foot-note the translation of passages in Greek in the text, in order that the main argument may not be obscured for readers unfamiliar with N. T. Greek,

II

PSYCHOTHERAPY—INTRODUCTION

THE employment of mental or spiritual means of healing, as opposed to those of drugs or the surgeon's knife, can be traced back to very early times. Indeed there are some who think that in the most primitive times those who practised the healing art used this method alone. Whether or not this be so it can be stated with considerable confidence that mental healing has been employed without intermission from the days when the celebrated method of 'incubation' was used in the temples of Asclepios down to the present day. Therapeutics of this kind have been connected through the centuries with religion, and have been received by the majority of men as something miraculous, in the sense of being the effect of the intervention of the deity or of some other superhuman being or beings. Only recently has psychotherapy come to be studied in a scientific spirit. This latter period may be said to begin with Mesmer and his followers at the end of the eighteenth and beginning of the nineteenth centuries. The growth in the understanding of the rationale of psychotherapy has been largely dependent upon the growth in the knowledge of morbid psychology, while the practice of the former has greatly facilitated insight into the latter—the two studies mutually interacting. Since psychotherapy as a science is still in its infancy, it is hardly surprising to find a great divergence of opinion amongst competent investigators as to the relative merits of the different methods practised, and a multitude of theories propounded to explain the facts which are observed. These conflicting views do not, however, much concern us in this essay. It is rather the observed facts which we need to consider—the theories being of secondary importance.

Although there are many differing schools of psychotherapy at the present time the differences between them are, apart from theories of mechanism, chiefly those of emphasis. Each school would admit the efficacy of the methods of the others under certain conditions. Some insist on the supreme value of the hypnotic trance for therapeutic purposes ; some think that 'suggestion' in the waking state or in an hypnoidal state, where the subject does not lose consciousness, is more effective ; others (e.g. Dubois and Déjerine)[1] prefer the method of 'persuasion' or rational appeal to the intelligence of the patient ; while yet others emphasize the primary importance of psycho-analysis as a healing agent. Probably the majority of practitioners employ a combination of all these methods, each showing a special preference for one or other of them. Thus Dr. J. A. Hadfield writes : 'Almost all methods, whether persuasion, drugs, suggestion, or analysis, are found to be efficacious in special cases, and it is the business of the psychotherapist, holding them all at his

---

[1] It is difficult to avoid the conviction that the 'persuasionists', for all their insistence on 'rational' treatment, do not eliminate 'suggestion' from their cures. For a criticism of Dubois's method by a protagonist of Freud's psycho-analytic method see Oskar Pfister (of Zurich), *The Psychoanalytic Method*, pp. 439-44 ; and for a criticism by one who practises hypnotism see Bonjour, *Les Guérisons miraculeuses modernes*, p. 39, n. 1.

disposal, to discover which is the most effective to apply to each type of case.'[1]

In order to show broadly what is meant by the term 'suggestion', and the distinction between the various forms of it, I cannot do better than quote again Dr. Hadfield. But first it must be remarked that the terminology used by psycho-therapists is by no means fixed, and that the same word may be employed by different writers to convey very varied shades of meaning, and sometimes even entirely different meanings. 'Suggestion', writes Dr. Hadfield, 'is the process by which ideas are introduced into the mind of a subject without being submitted to his critical judgment. The effect of any suggestion depends upon its evading the critical judgment of the reason.'[2]

'Waking suggestion depends for its force chiefly upon the authority of the physician and the expectancy of the patient, both of which factors tend to make the patient accept ideas without question or criticism. With a patient sufficiently suggestible, even in the fully waking state and though he has never been hypnotized, one can make the suggestion of anaesthesia, and then put a pin through his skin without producing the slightest pain ; or can compel him by waking suggestion to perform various movements. However hard the patient tries to act contrary to the suggestions, he finds that they dominate his mind and actions. The announcement, forcibly delivered to a paralytic patient in the waking state, that he can and will walk, sometimes produces the desired result, in some cases instantaneously. Such a patient is not to be considered a malingerer because he is cured by "stern" measures.'[3] 'The hypnoidal condition is one in which the patient's mind is put into a quiescent state, and rendered receptive and uncritical. In this state he hears and remembers

---

[1] *Functional Nerve Disease*, edited by Dr. Crichton Miller, p. 62.
[2] Ibid , p. 63. Cf. and contrast Prof. Charles Baudouin, *Suggestion and Autosuggestion*, p. 26 . 'Suggestion may be briefly defined as the subconscious realisation of an idea.' In heterosuggestion Baudouin recognizes two phases : (1) An idea, imposed by the operator, is accepted by the subject. This he calls 'acceptation'. (2) This idea undergoes transformation within the subject into the corresponding reality. This he calls the 'ideoreflex process' or 'autosuggestion' (op. cit., p 242).
[3] Ibid., p. 64.

all that the physican says, but does not concern himself to criticize the ideas, which therefore enter the mind as suggestions, and tend to work themselves out in thought, feeling, and action. . . . The essential difference between hypnoidal and hypnotic suggestion lies in the extent to which mental associations are still possible. The "depth" of the hypnosis depends on the relative inability to form associations with the other ideas and dispositions of the mind. There are times when hypnoidal suggestion, in which the paths of association with other dispositions of the mind are still to some extent left open, is more effective than hypnotic sugges- tion, in which almost complete dissociation is produced. In hypnoidal suggestion we may keep an idea, say that of "con- fidence ", dominant in the mind, and its influence will flow down, as it were, along the paths of association and over- whelm the other dispositions of the mind while these lie dormant and passive. In such a case, a condition of more complete dissociation, such as one gets in deep hypnosis, would be less effective, since the suggestion, before it could act on surrounding dispositions, would have to break down the barriers and resistances set up by the formation of the dissociation. This accounts for the fact that, in actual practice, treatment in the hypnoidal condition is often more successful than in the deep hypnotic. On the other hand, there are circumstances . . , in which deep hypnosis is preferable.' [1] The best single test, says Dr. Hadfield, of hypnosis as distinct from the hypnoidal condition is amnesia; but, he continues, 'it should be remembered by those who use waking or hypnoidal suggestion and decline to use hypnosis that the difference between these conditions is only a matter of degree, depending on the extent of dissociation '. [2]

It is often said that the number of people who can be hypnotized is very limited. Dr. Hadfield admits that a large number can never be made to ' lose consciousness ' or become amnesic. To gain some idea of the proportion of people who can be hypnotized he made the following experiment which I give in his own words : ' I hypnotized at once seventeen patients taken at random, and stuck a pin through a fold of skin in the hand of each one. As many as ten were found to

[1] Ibid., p. 64 f.   [2] Ibid., p. 66.

be amnesic, or " fast asleep ", to such a degree that, when they woke, they were unconscious of what I had done—i. e. they were in a condition of deep hypnosis. Of the remaining seven, six felt the putting in of the pin, but said they experienced no pain whatever—i. e. they were in a hypnoidal condition Only one out of the seventeen said he felt any pain, and he, curiously enough, ordinarily suffered from hysterical anaesthesia! Thus sixteen out of seventeen were analgesic and highly suggestible. A large majority of patients are sufficiently suggestible for treatment even though amnesia is not produced. The fact that the patient is "conscious" of what is said matters little, so long as he is not critical.' [1]

The stress which has been laid on the fact that the state of mind requisite for effective treatment by suggestion is one in which the patient is uncritical is something which, in considering the N.T. healing miracles, we need to mark carefully. The importance of it lies in this, that, if the above contention is true, it is not irrelevant to cite a modern instance of a cure brought about by the employment of deep hypnosis as being a possible parallel to a case of healing recorded in the N.T., even though our Lord and His followers never induced such a degree of hypnosis (and there is no evidence that they did this). It is interesting to observe in this connexion that recently a new school of psychotherapy has sprung up which calls itself the New Nancy School,[2] whose main distinguishing tenet may be put briefly by saying that it holds that the dominant factor in all suggestion is autosuggestion, and that, even in cases where deep hypnosis is 'induced' by an operator, the determining factor in the induction of this state is the subconscious (or unconscious) of the patient, i. e. the process should be more accurately described as autosuggestion.[3]

---

[1] *Functional Nerve Disease*, p 69 f. It should be noted that the experiment recorded above was made upon patients in a ' war-shock ' hospital, and therefore its results must not be taken as indicating the proportion of so-called ' normal ' subjects who can be hypnotized.

[2] The two chief representatives of this school are M. Émile Coué and Prof. Charles Baudouin. It has been said that these two stand in the same relation to the New Nancy School as Liébault and Bernheim stood to the (old) Nancy School. Coué has confined his attention chiefly to the practical working out of his theories, while Baudouin is the first theoretical exponent of the former's teaching.

[3] See Charles Baudouin, *Suggestion and Autosuggestion*, trans. by E. and C. Paul.

In order to make plain the essential unity of the phenomena under discussion it will be well to give one or two illustrations of the working of suggestion (using the term here to cover what is meant by auto- and hetero-suggestion in common parlance, and regardless of degree of hypnosis or 'awakeness').[1]

A good example to begin with may be taken from the curing of warts ; for, strangely enough, these seem to be peculiarly susceptible to mental treatment. 'In the Swiss canton of Vaud', says Prof. Baudouin, 'curers of warts abound ; and here it sometimes happens that the patient will employ a famous prescription without troubling to consult the healer. In these cases, autosuggestion is seen in all its beauty. Prescriptions pass from village to village and from hamlet to hamlet. Some of them are incredibly quaint. For example, to cause warts, the subject goes out one evening, moistens the tip of the finger, looks at a star, and simultaneously applies the wet finger-tip to the other hand. The operation is repeated, the finger being freshly moistened with saliva each time, while the subject counts "one, two, three, . ." up to the number of warts desired. Now, wherever the moistened finger-tip has been applied, a wart duly appears. I do not guarantee the alleged numerical precision, but the development of warts as the sequel of such practices is a proved fact. The Vaudois girls are very fond of this amusement—not for the mere pleasure of having warts (for the pleasure of their possession is certainly open to dispute), but for a pleasure which to them is very real and very great, the pleasure of passing them on to someone else. A ribbon is tied round the affected hand, and is knotted as many times as there are warts on the hand ; then the ribbon is dropped on the highway. Whoever picks it up and unties the knots, will get the warts, and the original owner of the warts will be cured. Another prescription, equally efficacious, is to rub the warts with a piece of bacon rind, which is subsequently placed beneath a stone, on damp ground. As soon as the bacon rind is rotten, the warts will be cured. But if, by bad luck, some-

---

[1] The illustrations that follow are, indeed, far removed from the recorded miracles in the N. T., but the relevance to our subject of the principles which they illustrate will be apparent in the sequel.

one moves the stone, one has wasted one's pains and one's bacon rind, and one must begin all over again.'[1]   Prof. Baudouin says, that 'the value of such methods depends upon their illogicality, their strangeness, which strikes the imagination of the simple, monopolises the attention, and fills the mind with a sense of mystery.'[2]

In the light of the above it is interesting to note that Dr. Bonjour of Lausanne cures severe cases of warts by suggestion, inducing in the patient for this purpose a light state of hypnosis (what he calls 'hypnosis of the first degree').[3]

Again, we may observe the power of suggestion to raise blisters. The example I shall cite gives some extremely interesting indications as to the part which pain plays in retarding the healing process. In recent years there has often been heated controversy as to whether it is possible to produce blisters on the skin by means of hypnotic suggestion alone. Here and there doctors have claimed to have done this,[4] but the soundness of the claim has not been universally admitted. During the war Dr. Hadfield, while serving as a surgeon in the Royal Navy, performed at Chatham a series of experiments upon a susceptible patient (' Leading Seaman H. P.') which has, I think, proved beyond cavil that blisters can be thus raised.[5]

In the first experiments Dr. Hadfield succeeded in producing blisters by suggesting to the hypnotized patient that he was being touched with a red-hot iron and that a blister would form as a result of this. He then proceeded to test the effect which pain had on his results, and he found that, if he touched a spot on the patient's arm with his finger suggesting

[1] Op. cit., p. 91.

[2] Ibid. Baudouin says also that in the same Swiss canton persons suffering from dropsy are cured by lying on two mattresses between which some toads have been placed.

[3] See Bonjour, *Les Guérisons miraculeuses modernes,* pp. 25-8, where he describes some cases in detail, giving pictorial and photographic illustrations. See also his table on pp. 44 and 45 of the same work.

[4] For example, Forel vouches for the justification of Wetterstrand's claim in two cases and that of Dr. Marcel Briand in a third. (See August Forel, *Hypnotism*, trans. by H. W. Armit, p. 112 f.)

[5] For the details of these experiments, and the precautions taken, I must refer to Dr. Hadfield's article in *The Lancet* for 3 Nov., 1917, entitled ' The Influence of Hypnotic Suggestion on Inflammatory Conditions'.

that he was touching it with a red-hot iron and causing pain, a blister duly formed ; but if he did the same thing with the suggestion this time that the patient would feel no pain no blister formed. After this he tried the effect of burning the patient in reality. I quote his own words : 'In the fifth and sixth experiments I actually burnt the patient during hypnosis with a hot iron—the end of a steel pencil-case heated in a Bunsen flame. In the fifth experiment (carried on simultaneously with the second) I suggested there should be no pain as a result of these burns. There was no pain either when the skin was touched or afterwards. But the remarkable thing was that in these burns there was no hyperaemia around. Round each of the two spots, which themselves presented the ordinary appearance of blisters, there was a thin red line and nothing more. These blisters healed very rapidly and never gave any sign of inflammation or pain.' Experiment 6 : 'Further, simultaneously with ex-periment 3 I made an actual burn and suggested pain—the condition, of course, which would occur in the normal waking state except that in this case the patient, being hypnotised, forgot all about it when he was "wakened". This continued to pain afterwards, and in this case there was very con-siderable hyperaemia, and the burn took longer to heal.'

In his conclusion Dr. Hadfield points out that these experi-ments were all in the sphere of non-bacteriological inflamma-tions. The exigencies of the Service prevented him at the time from experimenting with bacteriological inflammation. He holds that experiments 5 and 6 confirm the suggestions put forward by Hilton in his *Rest and Pain* that pain may act as a deterrent to healing. Pain, Dr. Hadfield says, is a very valuable indicator to point us to physical disorder or injury, but this seems to exhaust its function, and its aboli-tion, either by the surgical means suggested by Hilton or, if possible, by hypnotic means, would conduce to greater rapidity in healing. He also points out that these experi-ments in producing blisters indicate to what length the regu-lation of the blood-supply can go in a susceptible patient. Finally he says, ' This seems to indicate that when we know more about hypnotic suggestion, and have attained a greater skill in inducing it in a larger proportion of patients, we may be able to affect for good any organic inflammatory condition whether medical or surgical, both by regulating the blood-supply . . . and also by the abolition of pain.'

As a last example we may take a case of manifest auto-suggestion. It is one reported by Gillet, a pupil of Coué, and concerns an asthmatic who, on a holiday journey, was awakened during the night in his hotel by a violent paroxysm of his complaint. ' Greatly distressed for breath, he got out of bed and hunted for the matches. He had a craving for fresh air, but could not find the window. " Confound these third-rate hotels, where one gropes vainly in the dark ! " He is suffocating, and he clamours for air. Feeling about, he at length finds a pane of glass. '' Damn it all, where 's the window-bolt ? . . . Never mind, this will do ! " and he breaks the pane. The fragments fall to the floor. Now he can breathe ; again and again he fills his chest with the fresh air ; the throbbing at his temples passes, and he goes back to bed. " Saved ! ". . . Next morning, one of the items in his bill was, " Broken clock-case, fr. 4.35." ' [1]

For scientific treatment by psychotherapy it is necessary to understand the way in which diseases come about. It is to the psycho-analysts that we must turn for the modern theory of neuroses. For the main principles underlying this theory we are indebted to Prof. Freud of Vienna. This state-ment remains true in spite of the divergence (often very con-siderable) of the views of the schools, which have sprung up as the result of the initial impetus given by Freud, from those of Freud himself. For example, the debt to him is lasting, not only of Dr. Jung and the Zurich School but also of such thorough opponents as Dr. Alfred Adler and his followers. In this country the War has greatly stimulated the practice of psychotherapy, and the great number and variety of patients in our hospitals for ' shell-shock ' and war-neuroses have made possible a considerable advance both in theory and in methods of treatment. There would be few medical men who have benefited by this opportunity who would not admit that they owed much to Freud, although probably almost equally few would be whole-hearted followers of him. Thus many would part company with him in his insistence that the dominant

[1] Gillet, ' L'auto-suggestion,' *Bulletin École de Nancy*, 1913. I quote from Baudouin, op cit., p. 92.

and most determinative instinct in man is the sexual instinct and that all neuroses can be traced back to a sexual root.[1] Experience with numerous cases arising out of Active Service conditions has made this latter opinion difficult to hold, and has helped to confirm the opinion of those who would claim that there are other instincts no less fundamental than the sexual, and that they are capable of being quite as potent factors in the formation of a neurosis.[2] We need not, however, enter into a discussion on the conflicting views of psycho-analysts. For the purpose in hand it is sufficient to note certain outstanding factors in the 'mechanism' of hysteria[3] which are now generally, if not universally, recognized by those acquainted with the subject. The following terms (employed semi-technically) indicate briefly the process which is undergone in the production of an hysterical symptom. They are: 'complex', 'conflict', and 'repression'.

A 'complex' Dr. Bernard Hart describes as 'a system of connected ideas with a strong emotional tone and a tendency to produce actions of a certain definite character'.[4] Leading

[1] It is important to remember that in course of time Freud has given a wider and wider signification to the term 'Sexualitat', and that he distinguishes this term from 'Genitalitat'. (See 'Zur Psychoanalyse der Kriegsneurosen', *Internationale Psychoanalytische Bibliothek*, Nr. 1, p. 4 (1919).)

[2] On the nature and operation of the instincts, see Dr. McDougall's *An Introduction to Social Psychology*, 13th ed., pp. 19–89, 265-324, and 385 ff. On the 'herd instinct' in particular see W. Trotter, *Instincts of the Herd in Peace and War*.

[3] It is inevitable to employ the words 'hysteria' and 'hysterical', although one regrets doing so partly because of the diverse connotations which have been given to them and the fact that there is not even now a universally accepted definition of them, and partly because they have in the minds of most men outside of the medical profession a signification and associations which are entirely misleading now that they are no longer used solely in the restricted way of the earlier days of their employment. Dr. E. Prideaux (*Functional Nerve Disease*, ed. by Dr. Crichton Miller, p. 43) defines hysteria as 'a mental state manifesting itself by physical symptoms which can be removed by psychotherapy'. Cf. with this the definition of Dr. R. G. Gordon (*Seale Hayne Neurological Studies*, vol. i, Nr. 5, p. 264): 'Hysteria is a condition in which symptoms are present which are produced by suggestion and curable by psychotherapy.'

[4] *The Psychology of Insanity*, 3rd ed., p. 61. This description makes clear that there is nothing inherently morbid about a complex as such. In point of fact, however, the term is commonly used to designate an emotionally-toned system of ideas repressed into the unconscious (cf. Prideaux, op. cit, p. 48 f.). This seems to be the Freudian use of the term (cf. Bjerre, *The History and Practice of Psychanalysis*, p. 73).

up to an hysterical symptom may be found then this sequence: (1) A complex, being found incompatible with that which goes to make up the rest of the ego or with some other powerful complex or tendency of the ego, produces a 'conflict'. (2) The conflict may find a temporary or partial solution in the process which Freud calls 'Verdrängung',[1] or, as we say in English, 'repression' into the unconscious. This repression may, in different cases, be of varying degrees of completeness. (3) The complex thus repressed does not thereby cease to exist, nor does it cease to find expression, but is manifested in an 'hysterical symptom', which is thus an indirect expression of a repressed complex.[2] This manifestation is, as a rule, so 'camouflaged' that the person concerned entirely fails to recognize it for what it is. The hysterical symptom may be of many and various kinds. The factors which determine what form[3] it will take cannot all be enumerated with certainty, but it can be said with reasonable assurance that the form will depend partly upon the degree of repression attained and more especially upon the 'psychological type' to which the patient belongs.[4] Dr. Jung distinguishes two main psychological types, the 'extravert' type and the 'introvert' type.[5] An extravert is one in whom the affective side of his mental make-up is more fully developed than the cognitive side—his feelings are relatively well differentiated in comparison with his thinking. With the introvert, on the other hand, the cognitive element predominates over the affective—his thought is relatively well differentiated in comparison with his feeling.[6] These two types will be found to

---

[1] Cf. *Vorlesungen zur Einführung in die Psychoanalyse*, by Prof. Dr. Sigmund Freud, p. 334 f. (1918). See also *The History and Practice of Psychanalysis*, by Poul Bjerre, M.D., p. 73

[2] A complex may, of course, manifest itself in more than one hysterical symptom, and vice versa.

[3] I mean, e. g. worry and anxiety on the one hand or a functional paralysis on the other.

[4] As a matter of fact probably the degree of repression itself depends largely upon the 'psychological type'.

[5] See Jung, *Collected Papers on Analytical Psychology*, F. T, 2nd ed., pp. 287-98.

[6] Cf. Drs. Maurice Nicoll and James Young, *Functional Nerve Disease*, p. 144 f. According to them, a function that is relatively undifferentiated exists more beneath the level of consciousness than one that is well developed. 'Whatever exists in the unconscious is capable of producing neurosis, because

manifest two different kinds of hysterical symptoms, those of the former being distinguished under the name 'conversion hysteria', those of the latter under 'anxiety hysteria'[1]. The physical manifestations of 'conversion hysteria' reveal them-selves through the channels of the central nervous system, those of 'anxiety hysteria' for the most part through the channels of the autonomic nervous system. Dr. Prideaux says that in 'conversion hysteria' 'either no attempt is made to face the conflict, or there may be a short struggle corre-sponding with the period of meditation, and then the emotion attached to the complex becomes completely repressed and dissociated and gains expression, as in the child, through the channels of the central nervous system, but in an indirect way, so that its motive is not apparent to the personal con-sciousness.'[2] He proceeds to enumerate various factors which may determine the particular symptom. Thus, 'the emotion may simply fix symptoms which have already been produced as the result of emotional shock; for example, mutism, deaf-ness, blindness, and these symptoms become useful in that they prevent the patient from talking about, hearing about, or seeing, anything connected with his emotional experiences. It may fix symptoms due to actual physical trauma—for example, aphonia after gassing—or it may produce symptoms in some part to which attention has been drawn either at the time by a minor injury or at some earlier period by a previous accident; for instance, a slight bruise of the arm may be sufficient to cause an hysterical paralysis. . . . The

it is axiomatic that the neurosis is motivated from the unconscious.' 'The man whose feelings lie too much in the unconscious in an undifferentiated form would therefore develop an anxiety state under stress, while the man whose thinking, regarded as a function, remains largely at an unconscious level would develop a palsy. Jung regards neurotic breakdown as being due to the struggle between the differentiated function in consciousness with the undifferentiated function in the unconscious.' It must be remembered that the distinction of the two types is a broad one. Probably there is no single individual who is a com-plete 'extravert' or a complete 'introvert'. Moreover, it is not maintained here that a further division of types is not possible.

[1] This last is often somewhat misleadingly designated 'neurasthenia'. The discussion of the whole subject is greatly complicated by the variety of meanings attached to terms by different people. The terminology adopted above is that of Freud, and is one for which there seems hope of gaining general acceptance. See Prideaux, op. cit., p. 53 ff.

[2] Op. cit., p. 56.

determination of the symptom may also be due to the fact that the patient has seen or known of some one who has been through similar experiences and has suffered from some particular symptom as a consequence, so that he himself expresses his emotions in the same way by a method of sympathetic expression; many cases of hysterical stammering occur in this way. Another method . . . is that of "identification", in which the patient unconsciously identifies himself with some one whom he knew perhaps in childhood . . . whom he at one time wished to be like. If the person with whom he has identified himself had suffered from hemiplegia, then he would develop an hysterical hemiplegia.'[1]

With the foregoing it will be well to contrast the description that Dr. Prideaux gives of 'anxiety hysteria'[2]: 'In anxiety hysteria the social ideal at first tries to face the conflict, and only when it can no longer hold its own against the individual self is the complex repressed, and even then the repression appears to be incomplete. In these cases the patients generally tell us that they felt the symptoms coming on some time before they had their psychic trauma, and they generally recognize their previous conflict when it is presented to them, whereas the conversion case does not realize that he has ever had a conflict. The repressed emotion is directed along the paths of the autonomic nervous system, and the derangement of function of the viscera and endocrinic (*sic*) glands thus produced excites, by repercussion, a further emotional reaction with the production of anxiety. This anxiety cannot be attached to the repressed complex, and is

---

[1] Op. cit , p. 56 f. Cf. with this the six sets of circumstances which Dr. R. G. Gordon maintains will produce hysterical symptoms (*S. H. N. S.*, vol. 1, No. 5, p. 269 ff.) : (1) Found in people who have acquired a sense of inferiority either in respect of their whole body or of one or more limbs or organs. 'In such patients, who are almost hypochondriacal in their expectation of illness, the slightest physical accident or passing ache or pain is sufficient to determine an hysterical symptom either affecting the whole body or the particular limb or organ which is believed to be weak.' (2) Some actual physical trauma. (3) The stress of great emotion. (4) Hetero-suggestion—generally the result of some unwise remark or action. (5) Imitation. (6) 'Temporary organic disabilities which may range from blindness or deafness, through vomiting and urinary troubles, to paralysis, contractures, and anaesthesias.' These may produce habit continuations.

[2] Op. cit., p. 57 f.

consequently transferred to some other idea which is assimilable in consciousness. In this way are formed the numerous phobias from which these patients often suffer, and at the same time a vicious circle is set up. The nature of the phobia is determined by the conditions which were associated with the repressed complex ; thus if a child has been shut up in a cupboard, and there has been associated with this some mental conflict which has been repressed, then that child will be likely to develop claustrophobia.'

Enough has, I think, been said to indicate in very broad outline the theory of the mechanism of hysteria upon which 'modern psycho-analysts base their work.[1] Before the conclusion of these introductory remarks about psychotherapy there are a few further points to be taken into account. According to the Gospels it frequently happened that numbers of people suffering from various diseases flocked to Jesus, and He healed them.[2] Those who have held that the statements to this effect are merely inferences from the fact that Jesus cured certain individuals according to tradition may possibly have good grounds for their opinion, but their reasons certainly cannot be psychological ones. Whatever may be our views as to the mode of our Lord's healing activities, we shall not be disposed to deny that the laws of 'suggestion' were operative in His presence. It is an indisputable fact that one of these laws is that the suggestibility of individuals tends to be heightened in a crowd. Thus it is that doctors who practise hypnotic therapy are emphatic in their exposition of the merits of 'collective treatment'. For example, Dr. Hadfield advocates collective hypnosis not only because of the economy of time such a method makes possible, but also because of its more potent therapeutic effects. Collective treatment, he says, tends to encourage a 'curative atmosphere'. 'It enables us', he continues, 'to hypnotize patients very easily', for the suggestion of twenty men around in a condition of sleep is powerful enough to put a new

[1] For a lucid description of the chief factors in this mechanism, see Dr. Bernard Hart, *The Psychology of Insanity*, 3rd ed., pp. 58–116. On the whole theory cf. also Bjerre, op. cit., pp. 72–7, who gives examples from his own practice.

[2] Cf., e. g., Mk. iii. 7–11 and prls.; Mk. vi. 53–6, Mt. xiv. 34–6; Mt. xv. 29–31 ; Mk. i. 35–9 and prls., Mt. xiv. 13–14, Lk. ix. 10–11.

patient to sleep almost without further encouragement from the physician. The results I have recorded, which showed that sixteen out of seventeen patients became analgesic[1], are much more satisfactory than I could have obtained by treating the patients individually.'[2] The following is the way in which one of his patients, who was being treated for insomnia, described the influence of the collective hypnosis: 'On the occasions when I have been present at collective hypnosis there appeared to be a much stronger effect than when I was treated privately. The feeling I had on these occasions was, that the air was charged with sleep, and that drowsiness poured into one from all quarters instead of from one point only as in solitary treatment.'[3] As another example we may take the account which Dr. Poul Bjerre gives of what happened when Wetterstrand, inspired by Liébeault, took to employing hypnotic treatment. Previously he had practised on the ordinary medical lines of physicians, and had had a large clientèle. When he began his fresh departure by practising psychotherapy, 'it was', says Bjerre, 'as if a new Bethesda had suddenly arisen. The news spread throughout the town. A stream of sick people came from all directions. The consultation-room was besieged. People sat outside on the stairs and waited. It was no question of differentiation between functional and organic disease, between what could be attacked by this new method and what was inaccessible to it. Delighted over the possibilities that opened before him, Wetterstrand himself did not define so closely as he should have done, in order to preserve the reputation of his method of treatment. He seemed to believe that through suggestion both tumours and broken legs could be cured. Only by slow degrees did he learn the right indications.'[4] Bjerre goes on to say that Wetterstrand achieved the most surprising results. 'I have often heard', he says, 'from entirely reliable people case histories related which I could not have believed had they reached me in any other way.'[5]

---

[1] See above, p. 9 f.
[2] *Functional Nerve Disease*, p. 81.
[3] Ibid   [4] Bjerre, op. cit., p 39
[5] Ibid , p. 40.   Cf. with the two examples cited the account which Baudouin gives of Coué's collective sittings (*Suggestion and Autosuggestion*, p. 221).

From a psychological point of view, therefore, the reports of the healing of 'multitudes' by our Lord do not present great difficulties.

The mention of Wetterstrand's work serves to raise the vexed question as to whether or not it is possible for psychotherapy to remedy 'organic' disease as well as 'functional' disease. In this country and, for that matter, on the Continent and in America the medical profession generally (including that part of it which practises psychotherapy) would answer this in the negative. This fact, however, loses much of its significance when it is remembered that, according to the profession, a disease which has been cured by psychotherapy alone must be *eo ipso* a 'functional' disease.[1] The truth is that the boundary-line between 'functional' and 'organic' is so vague as to make either view plausible. The cases which are cited throughout this essay, and which are merely representative of many others, should make it clear that the term 'functional', if it is to be applied to them all, must have a very wide connotation. It is necessary to insist that, in adducing them as parallels to N. T. miracles, I am not thereby contending that the cases cured by our Lord were only 'hysterical'. Prof. Baudouin is one of the few who boldly assert the power of psychotherapy to cure at least some diseases which are definitely organic. The following passage from his book *Suggestion and Autosuggestion* leads one to suspect that he differs from the majority of those physicians who practise suggestion widely more in the matter of terminology than as regards facts. 'We have to note', he writes, 'that there is no radical difference between the action of suggestion when its results are purely functional, and its action when its results are organic. If we admit that suggestion can act in the former cases (and this has long been admitted), there need be no difficulty about acknowledging the reality of its action in the latter cases. For certain persons

---

[1] The religious associations for spiritual healing which attempt to work in conjunction with the medical profession are careful to limit their activities to 'functional' maladies. E.g., this is so of the 'Emmanuel Movement' in America (see *Religion and Medicine*, by Worcester, McComb, and Coriat, p. 4). Cf. also *Spiritual Healing*, being 'the report of a clerical and medical committee of inquiry into spiritual, faith, and mental healing', pp. 16 and 17. Cf. also the definitions of hysteria above, p. 15, note 3

. . . who regard as "incomprehensible" everything which
disturbs their habits of thought, the organic effects of suggestion are "inadmissible" until they have seen these effects
experimentally verified—and even thereafter.   Such persons
are extremely illogical.   They admit that suggestion acts on
the circulation, on the secretions, and in a localised fashion
upon various parts of the body, doing this through the inter-
mediation of the vasomotor nerves.   Now let us suppose that
the vasomotor mechanism stimulates or restricts the circulation
through the capillaries supplying some particular group of
cells, and that this action is *persistent.*   Thereupon the cells
of this group will, as the case may be, enjoy an excess of
nourishment, or will be insufficiently supplied.   They will
prosper, like parasites; or they will atrophy.   The suggestive
action which manifests itself in the case of tumours, local
malformations, &c, can be very simply explained on these
lines, without having recourse to any laws other than those
with which we are already familiar.'[1]

Note: During the course of this essay I shall take a considerable number of my illustrations from cases arising out of
war conditions on the battlefield.   The reason for this is partly
because such case-histories are more accessible than civilian
ones, and partly because they are, as a rule, of comparatively
simple aetiology and character, thus making it possible to
study the mechanism of the psychoneuroses, as Dr. Hadfield
says, 'almost under laboratory conditions'.[2]   It cannot, however, be urged too strongly that this mechanism does not need
the detonation of high explosives to set it in motion.[3]

[1] P. 102.   See also p. 23.   Cf Bjerre (op cit, p. 37), who thinks that there
is often a real truth underlying the persistent exclamation of people who, though
they may have all possible respect for the bacillus of tuberculosis and know
what mischief it produces, yet say, 'He *worried* himself into consumption '.

[2] *Functional Nerve Disease,* p 62.

[3] Cf. Dr M. D. Eder, *War-Shock,* p. 145: ' War-shock is not a new disease ·
it is a variety of hysteria where the one factor (the psychic trauma) is over-
whelmingly large in relation to the second factor (predisposition); it is separated
from non war-shock cases in degree, not in essence'.   Cf. also Freud, 'Zur
Psychoanalyse der Kriegsneurosen,' *Internationale Psychoanalytische Bibliothek,*
Nr. 1, p. 6 (1919).

III

A. THE SYNOPTIC GOSPELS

In attempting to conjure up afresh the scenes of our Master's healing ministry we are bound, if we intend our picture to be other than purely fanciful, to remain faithful to the documents which provide us with the most satisfactory data available for this purpose. But our documents, although they may contain reminiscences of eye-witnesses of the scenes described, are not themselves contemporary records of the events which they narrate; moreover it is obvious that their authors wrote with a purpose, and made no attempt to provide their readers with dry and precise details which seemed to have no bearing on their Christian life and profession. As Dr. Georges Berguer says of the Gospels: 'ils ne sont pas *historiques* au sens propre du mot, c'est-à-dire qu'il ne rentre pas dans l'intention de leurs auteurs de faire de l'histoire désintéressée, avec un souci primordial d'exactitude historique. Ce sont bien plutôt des ouvrages *d'édification.*'[1] Evidence of this stands out clearly in the healing narratives. The age in which the Evangelists wrote was not a scientific one, and the reports of the working of marvels or of wonderful cures did not present any difficulties to ordinary folk. Hence we find again and again in the Gospels that where scenes are described in which Jesus cured people who were sick the centre of interest is not on the details of the healing (as it would be nowadays) but on some controversy (as for example the Sabbath controversy) associated with the event which was of deep concern to the earliest Christian communities. On this account we are supplied for the most part with very scant information about the nature of the diseases treated and the circumstances attending the healing processes. In any effort, therefore, to reconstruct with approximate accuracy the

---

[1] *Quelques traits de la Vie de Jésus au point de vue psychologique et psychanalytique* (1920), Introduction, p. lxxix.

incidents thus vaguely recorded it will be necessary to take
into consideration not only the data provided by a critical
estimate of the documents but also so far as is possible the
psychology of the community in and for which the authors
wrote.

There is little need in this essay to go minutely into the
Synoptic Problem. The accounts of the healing miracles
strongly support the contention of almost all present-day critics
of the Synoptics that Mt. and Lk. in writing their Gospels
employed an edition of Mk. which differs, if it differs at all,
only slightly from our own. An examination of these miracles
makes it difficult to avoid the conviction that Mk., in the cases
which he describes, gives us as a general rule the most
primitive extant narrative of events. I have indicated the
reasons for this statement when dealing with individual
miracles.

A word should be said about the alleged medical language
of Lk. For a considerable time in my study of the miracles
of healing in the Synoptics I assumed the substantial correctness of Hobart's thesis [1] that Lk. employed to a very large
extent technical medical terminology. The problem then
presented itself as to how Lk. could be so medical in his
language and so unmedical in his diagnosis as he often
appeared to be. For example, in the case of Peter's mother-
in-law, Mk. i. 30 describes her as πυρέσσουσα, and Lk. iv. 38 as
συνεχομένη πυρετῷ μεγάλῳ. Hobart shows that συνέχεσθαι is
used by the medical writers as in this passage in Lk., and
that they distinguish between πυρετὸς μέγας and πυρετὸς μικρός.[2]
He argues that Lk. is employing precise medical terminology,
while Mk. (and Mt.) gives merely a general popular description
of the disease. If this is so it is hard to understand why,
when we come to the accounts of the cure, we find that Lk is
much more 'unscientific' than Mk. Speaking of Jesus Mk.
i. 31 says, καὶ προσελθὼν ἤγειρεν αὐτὴν κρατήσας τῆς χειρός: Lk.
iv. 39 says, καὶ ἐπιστὰς ἐπάνω αὐτῆς ἐπετίμησεν [3] τῷ πυρετῷ. That
is to say, according to Lk., Jesus treated the case as though
it was one of demon possession. A medical man brought up
in the tradition of Hippocrates would not be likely to record

---

[1] *The Medical Language of St. Luke* (1882).
[2] Ibid., p. 3.   [3] Cf. Mk. i. 25; ix. 25, &c

a diagnosis of this kind unless he felt bound to do so. In this instance Mk.'s version shows that there was no such necessity.

The perplexity resulting from this apparent contradiction turns out to be unnecessary. The recently published comparison of Lk. with the LXX, Josephus, Plutarch, and Lucian (most minutely the last) by Prof. Henry J. Cadbury makes it difficult to doubt that there is nothing ·peculiarly technical about Lk.'s vocabulary his language is more literary than that of the other Evangelists, but it is not more technical.[1] Therefore, although the writer of the third Gospel (and Acts) may have been a doctor, the literary evidence does not prove that he was one trained in the scientific Hippocratic school, while his accounts of miracles tend to indicate that he was not nurtured in this tradition.

B. THE FOURTH GOSPEL.

It is a commonplace that on moving from the Synoptics to the Fourth Gospel we come into a strikingly different atmosphere of thought and outlook. Nowhere is this more apparent than in the treatment of miracles. In the Synoptics we see Jesus working miracles almost reluctantly, and generally refusing to perform the marvellous simply as a sign (cf., e.g., Mk. viii. 11, 12), and yet, through sheer sympathy and compassion, constantly giving evidences of His power; in John, on the contrary, only a few miracles are recorded, and these are for the most part of an especially wonderful

[1] See H. J. Cadbury, *Harvard Theological Studies*, VI. i, 'The Diction of Luke and Acts.' pp. 39-72. N B. the following by Prof G. F. Moore in a note (p 53 f)· 'Modern medical terminology is a barbarous artificial jargon, consisting partly of terms that have come down from the Greeks, in Greek or translated into Latin, partly of invented terms, coined after the pattern of the ancient, in a Greek or Latin which is often palpably counterfeit Many medical terms, especially the older ones, have come into common use, frequently supplanting ... native English words that mean exactly the same thing; and in recent times various agencies of vulgarization have made the lay public acquainted with hundreds of doctor's words, which they use—or abuse—with a self-satisfied feeling that they are talking the professional lingo. Greek scientific terminology is the contrary of all this. Its technical terms are native, not foreign; they were not invented, but were real words of the living language. and in considerable part the everyday names for the thing, more exactly defined, if necessary, but not diverted from their meaning.'

nature, and are represented as having been worked as signs with a very definite evidential purpose. Again, in the Synoptics it is urged with reiterated insistence that miracle is only possible if there is an antecedent faith, while in John it is the miracle that induces the faith—i. e., the miracle comes first, the faith afterwards, and as a result of it.[1]

It is not possible within the limits of this essay to discuss adequately even the main problems which the Fourth Gospel presents. There is much in it that seems entirely incompatible with the Synoptic record ; on the other hand, it contains many minute and accurate details (especially about places) which, to say the least, warn us against setting down the descriptions of scenes as all being undoubtedly the work of a late writer who has relied upon vague traditions and his own imagination.

The difficulties which have been indicated briefly above show clearly, I think, that, since the Johannine evidence in respect of the method of healing is of very uncertain value, no useful purpose will be gained from the point of view of the present study by examining in detail the healing works in the Fourth Gospel and by attempting to adduce modern parallels. I am therefore omitting to deal with them in this way, both for the general reasons already stated, and also because even a superficial examination of John's healing miracles induces one to suspect that they are (with the exception, perhaps, of the raising of Lazarus) very possibly different versions of miracles already recorded by the Synoptists.

The cases of healing in John are four in number (if we include the raising of Lazarus under this head) :

(1) Cure of the son of a courtier (τις βασιλικός) in Galilee (Jn. iv. 46-54). There can be little doubt that this is another version of the (? Q) story of the Centurion's Servant (Mt. viii. 5-13 ; Lk. vii. 1-10). According to all three Evangelists the cure is worked from a distance. · We are unable to say with certainty from what disease the patient was suffering. Lk. describes him as very ill, and at the point of death ; Mt. says he was suffering from paralysis, and in terrible agony (παραλυτικός, δεινῶς βασανιζόμενος). Jn. says he was at the

---

[1] Jn. is not, however, without an echo of the Synoptic record that preliminary faith is necessary. Cf., e. g., Jn. iv. 50.

point of death, and mentions incidentally that he had been suffering from fever (πυρετός v. 52).[1]

(2) The lame man at the pool of Bethesda (Jn. v). There are in this account minute details of place and scene the probable accuracy of which is coming to be admitted.[2] Whether the event described actually took place in this setting we have no means of judging until more is known of Jn.'s historical trustworthiness. There is nothing *a priori* improbable about its main features. Vv. 8 and 9 are reminiscent of the Synoptic account of the Capernaum paralytic.

(3) The man born blind (Jn. ix.) There are obvious points of contact between this story and that of the blind man of Bethsaida (Mk. viii 22-26). If the man was born blind it would be hard to find a fully accredited modern parallel to his healing.

(4) The raising of Lazarus (Jn. xi. 1-44 ff.). Of all the N. T. miracles (with the exception of the so-called nature-miracles) this is the one that most strains the credence of those who wish to believe in their historicity. Apart from the (to the modern mind) extreme *a priori* improbability of the story, many arguments have been brought forward to show that the whole account is fictitious. The strongest and most plausible is the argument from the silence of the Synoptists. It is urged that such an astounding miracle could not but have been known by all and recorded by the Synoptic Evangelists if it had occurred. Again, those who use this argument go on to say that Jn. makes the Lazarus incident the chief event that led to our Lord's arrest and trial; that, having inserted earlier the story of the cleansing of the Temple (which holds this position in the Synoptists), he employed the Lazarus narrative as an effective substitute for it; and that, if this incident really was the critical one which it is made to appear to be, it is inconceivable that the Synoptists would have omitted it. I do not think that these arguments are as convincing as at first sight they may appear to be. For

---

[1] Dr. E. A. Abbott suggests that Jn. is deliberately correcting Mt., and that Mt. is in error from having confused πυρετός with πάρετος (see *The Fourfold Gospel*, Sect. III, p. 198).
[2] See the extremely interesting discussion on this by Dr. Rendel Harris, *Side-lights on N. T. Research*, Lect. II and Appendix.

example, to those who believed in the restoration to life of Jairus's daughter and possibly the boy of Nain, would the raising of Lazarus appear anything more exceptionally extraordinary? Further, it seems to me that undue emphasis is laid upon the position which the Lazarus story holds in Jn. There are frequent indications elsewhere in this Gospel that Jesus was in serious danger from certain sections of the community, and in the story of Lazarus itself, before the miracle has taken place, it is made patent that Jesus would have been in considerable peril were He to come up into the neighbourhood of Jerusalem. It may well be that His delaying two days after He had heard the news of Lazarus' illness should be interpreted as due to His requiring to make sure of the will of God that He should so early endanger His life for the sake of His friends. The story makes it clear enough that personally it must have been His wish to go to the help of Mary and Martha and their brother. When finally He decided to go, Thomas speaks to his fellow-disciples and says, 'We too will go, that we may die with him' (i. e., no doubt, with Jesus).[1] Jn. really gives the impression that the mere presence of our Lord in Jerusalem would be sufficient to bring about His arrest, and that such a dramatic event as the raising of Lazarus, though naturally hastening it, was by no means necessary for it. Taking into account the remarkable vividness of the story, and the fact that the Synoptists imply a longer ministry in the neighbourhood of Jerusalem than they actually record, we may well believe that there is at least a sound substratum of truth underlying this Johannine narrative.

C. THE 'ACTS'

It is not possible in this essay to enter into a discussion of the often complicated analyses of the sources of this book which have been proposed by various scholars. There is a fairly general consensus of opinion that the third Gospel and Acts are the work of one man. That the author was the St. Luke of tradition appears to me by far the most

---

[1] *v.* 16. Cf. *v.* 8.

probable of hypotheses; as Mr. J. M. Thompson says, 'the
Lucan authorship would not have been seriously doubted
unless it had been traditional'.[1] This, however, is not to
say that the evidential value of every part of his writings is
of equal worth Lk. as an historian uses sources (following
them as a rule it would seem remarkably closely [2]) but unfortunately there is little evidence that he selected them in a very
critical spirit. Just as in the Lucan Gospel we can detect
different strata of tradition, so here certain clear divisions
may be observed. Thus the book may be divided into two
halves, the first i–xv. 35, and the second xv. 36 to the end.
The first deals primarily with the church in Jerusalem, the
second confines its attentions solely to St. Paul and his
doings, and includes what is known as the 'we-sections',
which are apparently extracts from the journal of an eye-
witness who may be supposed with reasonable probability to
be the author of the whole work.

The most common view respecting the Judean section
which has obtained of late years is that it is composed from
various sources, written or oral, or both, which are of varying
and doubtful worth.[3] The recent researches, however, of
Prof. C. C. Torrey of Yale have shown that it may be held
with a considerable degree of plausibility that the whole
of this section is a translation from a single Aramaic document.[4] Prof. Torrey maintains that the author of the Greek
half of the book composed his narrative as the continuation
of the Aramaic document.[5] He goes on to argue for 64 as
being the probable date of the writing of chs. xvi–xxviii, and
late 49 or early 50 for the Aramaic document.[6] If we accept
the possibility of the correctness of his theory (and his argument is no weak one) it will be necessary, while still remaining
in doubt about the full evidential value of the Judean section
(especially the miraculous element in it—such stories are
liable to grow with remarkable rapidity), to avoid rejecting
the evidence as certainly untrustworthy.

[1] *M. N T.*, p 113
[2] Cf. Prof. Charles Cutler Torrey, 'The Composition and Date of Acts'
Harvard Theological Studies, 1916–18, 1), p. 40
[3] Cf. Moffatt, *I. L. N. F.*, p. 290.
[4] See C. C. Torrey, 'The Composition and Date of Acts,' op. cit.
[5] Op. cit , p. 40.   [6] Op. cit., p. 67 f.

If we take Harnack's tabulation [1] of the summary accounts of miracles and the records of particular cures worked through members of the Christian community we observe the interesting fact that they all, with only one exception (and that not a specific record ; xix. 11 f.), fall within either the Judean section (chs. i–xv) or the 'we-sections'. The division is as follows :

I. Summary accounts of miracles (which we may place under the general heading of σημεῖα, τέρατα, δινάμεις) :

Chs. i–xv.   8
'We-sections'   1

II. Specific instances of healing :

Chs. i–xv.   .   .   .   .   5 (or 6, if we include xiv. 19 f.)
'We-sections'   .   .   .   4

It is, however, necessary to bear in mind that of the special instances in the 'we-sections' in two cases the account of the cure itself is not definitely written by one who was actually present. Thus in the case of the 'possessed' slave-girl (xvi. 16 ff.) we cannot be sure that the description of the healing formed part of the journal, and in that of Eutychus (xx. 9 f.) the writer of the journal makes it fairly clear that he was not present (see ver. 13).[2]

To summarize : The evidence for works of healing in the Acts is confined almost exclusively to the Judean section and to the 'we-sections' ; moreover the latter provide us with evidence of a relatively high order while that of the former is not so negligible as has often been supposed.[3]

[1] Harnack, *The Acts of the Apostles*, p. 134 f.
[2] Cf. J. M. Thompson, *M N. T.*, p. 114 f.
[3] The seemingly somewhat artificial parallelism between the acts and experiences of Peter and Paul noted by Prof P. W. Schmiedel (*E. B.* 41) ought to be taken into account, but I do not think it materially affects the statement made above.

IV

CURRENT BELIEFS LIABLE TO AFFECT DIAGNOSIS OF DISEASE AND METHODS OF HEALING

A. *Relation between Sin and Suffering*

In the O. T. the early, and throughout dominant, belief was that suffering and disease were due to sin. This doctrine is enunciated unequivocally in Lev. xxvi and the parallels in Deuteronomy (e. g. Deut. xxviii. 15 ff.). No less clear is Exod. xv. 26: 'If thou wilt diligently hearken to the voice of the Lord thy God, and wilt do that which is right in his sight, and wilt give ear to his commandments, and keep all his statutes, I will put none of these diseases (מַחֲלָה) upon thee, which I have brought upon the Egyptians: for I am the Lord that healeth thee.' This predominant belief can be traced from early times down through the later literature (e. g., Ps. vi, xxxii, xxxviii, li, cii; Ecclus. xxxviii) to the literature of Rabbinic Judaism, where the belief in 'Measure for Measure' is widely prevalent. Thus R. Jonathan said: 'Diseases (נְגָעִים) come for seven sins: for slander, shedding blood, false oaths, unchastity, arrogance, robbery, and envy' ('Erachin, 16 a).[1] According to 'Leviticus Rabba' (xviii, § 4) leprosy was the result of slander. On the other hand 'When Israel stood round Sinai and said, All that the Lord has spoken we will do, there was among the people no one who was a leper, or blind, or halt, or deaf,' &c. (ibid.).[2] These examples from Rabbinic literature can be multiplied.[3]

On the other hand there are not wanting in the O. T. indications that the belief in the connexion of sin and disease was not universally accepted. The contrary is emphasized

---

[1] Israel Abrahams, *Studies in Pharisaism and the Gospels*, First Series, ch. xiii.

[2] Abrahams, ibid.

[3] See Abrahams, ibid and Schechter, *Studies in Judaism*, pp. 260-75.

in the Book of Job.[1]   That the writer of Job was expressing
an individual and original conception is *a priori* improbable.
In any event his writing no doubt influenced subsequent
Jewish thought.   The sufferings of the Jewish people in
their later history must have made the old belief in all its
rigidity extremely difficult to hold.   Was Israel so much
worse than its heathen neighbours?   In all equity, did it
deserve such a heavy proportion of afflictions?   There is
ample evidence that the problem was felt to be acute by
thinking men.[2]   Attempts were made to modify, tone down,
and explain away the full force of the original doctrine.   It
is difficult to believe that some did not find light in the
attitude adopted in the book of Job.   That there was a continuous tradition of this kind can hardly be proved, but there
are hints that such may have existed.   Ps. lxxiii, xxxvii, and
xlix are examples of this trend of thought[3]   In Prov. iii. 11,
12 we have a modification of the early doctrine along the
lines of the argument of Eliphaz in Job v. 17, but it is not the
full radical doctrine of Job.   In the Rabbinical writings
this view is held by so great an authority as R. Meir, who
altogether disputed the theory as to the connexion between
suffering and transgression.   He held that God's dealing
with men was an unfathomable mystery.[4]   Dr. Schechter[5]
quoting from passages in 'Sabbath' 55 b, and 'Menachoth'
29 b, says, 'one gains the impression that some Rabbis rather
·thought that this great problem will indeed not bear discussion
or solution at all'.   However, it is precarious to argue from
the Babylonian Talmud as to beliefs in the time of our Lord.

   That this old question was still exercising men's minds
during the N. T. period is evident.   Mr. Montefiore, com-
menting on Mk. ii. 1–12, says, 'Jesus adopts the current

---

   [1] ? First half of fifth century, B C. (Duhm) or about the close of the fifth
century or later (see A. S Peake, *P. C.*, p 346).   Dr. G. Buchanan Gray says :
' Job is best explained as the product of a period lying between the close of
the seventh and the beginning of the second century B. C., and indeed at some
distance from either of these extreme limits'.   On the whole he thinks the
evidence points to the fifth century (see 'Job' by Driver and Gray, *Inter-
national Critical Commentary*, Introduction, p. lxix f. [1921].)
   [2] See Schechter, op. cit., p. 264 ff.
   [3] Cf. Prof. W. G. Jordan, *P. C* , p. 93
   [4] Abrahams, op. cit., ch. xiii ; cf. Schechter, op. cit., p. 275 .
   [5] Op. cit., p. 276.

view that the malady is the result of sin. Nor, however much some theologians would desire it, does he ever really combat the doctrine, false and strange as it seems to us, that disease implies sin. The theologians quote Lk. xiii. 1-5 and Jn. ix. 2 ; but the second passage is not in point, and in fact is the exception which proves the rule, while the first cannot surely be said to prove so large and revolutionary a doctrine.'[1] Mr. Montefiore is hardly justified in these assertions. The direct evidence is indeed limited, but, so far as it goes, it points to the fact that our Lord at no time taught definitely the doctrine of the relation between sin and physical disaster, but on the other hand did 'really combat' that doctrine. The argument that He held that belief is based on the incident of the paralytic (Mk. ii. 1-12 and-prls.), and also, presumably, on Jn. v. 14, reinforced by the *a priori* assumption that He would hold such a doctrine 'with the majority of his contemporaries'.[2] But the words in Mk. ii. 5 and prls. do not necessarily imply this interpretation. It is not prima facie obvious that there is here any connexion between the forgiveness of sins and the healing, or the sins and the disease, although as a matter of fact I think (and attempt to show below when dealing with the miracle) that there is such a connexion, and that this particular malady was caused by sin or, more accurately, the consciousness of sin. But, taking this latter view, we are not warranted in inferring that our Lord attributed to sin or sins diseases in general. Jn. v. 14 certainly does suggest that Jesus shared the prevalent opinion on this matter, but there seems to me too great a similarity between this miracle and that of the paralytic in the Synoptics to justify us in laying stress upon it. Mr. Montefiore says that Jn. ix. 2 is not in point—yet surely it is. Has not the extreme case of a man born blind been inserted largely because it is in itself a *reductio ad absurdum* of the doctrine commonly accepted? The explanation given in Jn. is that the man was born blind ἵνα φανερωθῇ τὰ ἔργα τοῦ θεοῦ ἐν αὐτῷ, with which we may compare the words with regard to Lazarus (xi. 4) Αὕτη ἡ ἀσθένεια οὐκ ἔστιν πρὸς θάνατον ἀλλ' ὑπὲρ τῆς δόξης τοῦ θεοῦ, ἵνα δοξασθῇ ὁ υἱὸς τοῦ θεοῦ δι' αὐτῆς. The Lazarus narrative tells, by implica-

---

[1] C. G. Montefiore, *The Synoptic Gospels*, vol. i, p. 77.
[2] Montefiore, op. cit., Introduction, p. lxxxviii.

tion, as much against the prevalent belief about sin and
disease as does that of the man born blind.   Of course we may
rule out of court Johannine evidence, but then Jn. v. 14 must
go along with the rest.   There remains the section peculiar
to Lk. (xiii. 1–5).   It is true that it is not in itself sufficient
to prove that our Lord held the doctrine in question.   It
cannot, however, be ignored.   We shall probably attach
greater or less weight to it according to our general estimate
of the character of our Lord on other grounds.   We are at
least not justified in assuming, without much more cogent
arguments than have been adduced, that He did hold the
view of 'the majority of His contemporaries'.

B.   *Belief in Demons*

It is difficult to estimate accurately the extent of the belief
in demons in Palestine in the time of our Lord.   The
Synoptic Gospels are in themselves sufficient evidence that
such a belief did exist at that time.   No sober criticism will
maintain that all the references in the Synoptics to demons
and unclean spirits are simply due to the influence of later
ideas.   But there are some scholars who hold that the
extent of this belief is as a rule greatly exaggerated.   Thus
Mr. Loewe [1] while admitting the belief in the existence of
spirits maintains that it was largely limited to Galilee and
Babylonia.   Palestine, he says, on the whole was free from
it.   He notes the different attitudes adopted by the Rabbis
according to Talmudic evidence, and that it will 'almost
invariably' be found there that Galilean teachers accepted,
while Judean teachers rejected, the belief.   Mr. Abrahams [2]
takes a similar line.   His argument deserves examination.
Demoniac possession, he says, as a cause of disease, and
exorcism as its cure, were well known to the Rabbis.   'But
it is certain that these beliefs and practices were uncommon
in Palestine at the time of Jesus.   The easy assumption to
the contrary has no foundation.'   He goes on to point out

[1] Herbert Loewe, art. 'Demons and Spirits' (Jewish), *E. R. E.*
[2] Abrahams, op. cit., ch. xiii.

that, though the Enoch and other Apocalyptic literature has a developed demonology and Acts xxiii. 8 implies a Pharisaic angelology, there is a remarkable infrequency of references to the subject in the Mishnah and Tannaite literature.[1] Hillel, he continues, was a student of demon-lore, perhaps under Parsic influence, but was by birth a Babylonian. Members of the Sanhedrin were expected to understand magic in order to deal with causes in which the question arose.[2] The Mishnah (Aboth, v. 9) refers to demons, but this, like Hagigah 16 a, apparently belongs to the late second century. ' It is in the Babylonian Talmud that we find an appalling mass of demonology which, though it stands in relation to earlier beliefs—Biblical, Apocalyptic, and Rabbinical—cannot properly be cited as applicable to the time of Jesus in the Holy Land.' Mr. Abrahams further points out that between 150 and 450 there was a great increase in Jewish circles in the belief in demons and their influence. He admits that some cases of exorcism are recorded earlier, but emphasizes that they are all associated with the Roman imperial family. 'Josephus, who makes indeed a general assertion as to demoniac possession,[3] only recites an actual cure by exorcism performed in the presence of Vespasian.'[4] With regard to the Jewish exorcists mentioned in Acts xix. 13 he says that the impression conveyed is that they were playing with foreign fire.[5] '

In this argument too much has had to be admitted on the opposite side to make the conclusion reached quite satisfactory. A developed demonology in the Enoch and other Apocalyptic literature (in so far as this literature is pre-Christian) cannot have been without considerable influence on Palestinian thought.[6] Again, although Hillel was by birth a Babylonian, it must be remembered that he almost certainly spent the

---

[1] He refers to L. Blau, *Das altjudische Zauberwesen*, p. 23.
[2] Sanhedrin 17 a. See refs. in Taylor, Aboth, v. 9.
[3] *Wars*, VII. vi. 3.
[4] *Antiquities*, VIII. ii. 5.
[5] He refers to Kohler, *J. E.* iv. 517 b.
[6] For the influence of Enoch upon the N. T. see Charles, *Apocrypha and Pseudepigrapha of the O. T.*, vol. II, p. 180 f. ; for the features of N. T. demonology which first appear in Enoch, ibid., p. 185. See also F. C. Conybeare, *J. Q. R.*, vol ix, p. 75 f.

main part of his life in Jerusalem, and that at a period prior
to our Lord's ministry.[1]　Mr. Abrahams is right in denying
the applicability of the appalling mass of demonology in the
Babylonian Talmud,[2] but at the same time he admits that it
stands in some relation to earlier Biblical, Apocalyptic, and
Rabbinical beliefs.　The paucity of references to evil spirits
in the O. T. is certainly significant.　In 1 Sam. xvi. 14-23,
xviii. 10, xix. 9 we have an account of the 'evil spirit from
the Lord' (&c. רוּחַ־רָעָה מֵאֵת יהוה) which possessed Saul, and
which David exorcized with music.[3]　In Judges ix. 23 we
read that 'God sent an evil spirit (וַיִּשְׁלַח אֱלֹהִים רוּחַ רָעָה) between
Abimelech and the men of Shechem', so that 'the men of
Shechem dealt treacherously with Abimelech'.[4]　In 1 Kings
xxii. 19-23 there is an account of the 'lying Spirit' (רוּחַ שֶׁקֶר)
which misled the prophets of Ahab.　Ver. 23 runs: 'Now
therefore, behold, the Lord hath put a lying spirit in the
mouth of all these thy prophets, and the Lord hath spoken
evil concerning thee.'[5]　It is noteworthy that in all these
passages the evil spirit is sent by Yahweh.　Whether this
was so in the original sources must be doubtful, but it is good
evidence as to the attitude of the compilers of the books as
we have them.　The evidence points in the direction of an
angelology rather than a demonology.　This distinction is
an important one, for although the two inevitably tend to
coalesce it would seem that they start from two entirely
different notions.　An angelology starts from a belief in
a transcendent God and the necessity for intermediate beings

---

[1] See W. Bacher, art. 'Hillel', *J. E.*

[2] Dr. Menzies Alexander, *Demonic Possession in the N. T.* (1902), p. 25 ff.
errs completely in this respect.

[3] Dr. W. H. Bennett, *P. C.*, ad loc., attributes xvi. 14-23 to J, xviii. 10 to
R, and xix. 9 to E.　By J and E he refers to sections similar to the Penta-
teuchal J and E. material (*P. C.*, p. 273).

[4] It is impossible to say whether the reference to the 'evil spirit' belongs to
the primitive source or to 'D'.

[5] It is difficult to estimate the date of this passage.　The book throughout is
Deuteronomic in tone and structure (see Dr. Foakes Jackson, *P. C.*, p. 294)
Dr. Skinner (1 and 2 Kings, *Cent. Bib.*, p. 28 f.) thinks this passage is taken
from a group of northern narratives mainly of a political character.　There is
a striking similarity between xxii. 19 ff. and Job i. 6 ff.　Probably these ideas
are comparatively late among the Hebrews.

between Him and mankind,[1] while a demonology has its
roots in primitive animistic beliefs.[2] The Satan of Job i. 6 ff.
is a good example of the tendency of the two to coalesce.[3]
There is in the O. T. a considerable amount of reference
to angels[4] and a certain amount of semi-angelology of the
kind just dealt with (cf. e.g. Isa. xix. 14; Zech. iii. 1, 2).
But all this is in marked contrast to the demonology of
such writings as, for example, Tobit vi, viii. 3. There
is, however, also evidence that the Hebrews were in danger
of succumbing to the demonic beliefs of their neighbours.
As the prophets amply testify, there was a continual tendency to forsake Yahweh and to turn to heathen cults and
practices—and these often of an animistic nature. In Lev.
xvii. 7 we read[5]: 'And they shall no more sacrifice their
sacrifices unto the שְׂעִירִם, after whom they go a whoring.' (Cf.
the שְׂעִירִים in Isa. xiii. 21.) 'Satyrs' were apparently 'goat-
shaped demons of the desert, the Hebrew counterparts of
the Arabian "jinn", and of the satyrs and fauns of classical

---

[1] I do not, of course, mean that belief in a transcendent God belongs to a
very primitive stratum of belief. Ultimately, no doubt, the source or sources of
angelology and demonology are the same. See Robertson Smith, *Rel. of Sem.*
(new ed. 1894), pp. 119-39, and 441 ff.; also Bousset, *Die Religion des
Judentums*, p. 334. It is interesting to note that there is to be found in modern
India a distinction similar to the one which I have drawn above. I quote from
W. T. Elmore, 'Dravidian Gods in Modern Hinduism' (reprinted from the
University Studies of the University of Nebraska, vol. xv, No. 1, 1915), p. 51,
note 1 · 'Brahmanic Hinduism is not lacking in demons. The "Rakshasas"
of the Rigveda are demons. There is, however, a marked distinction between
the demons of Hinduism and the Dravidian demons. . . The most persistent
distinction is that the "Rakshasas" and Hindu demons have a divine origin,
while the Dravidian demons usnally are the spirits of dead people . . . There
is considerable confusion concerning these two classes of demons, not only in
books on Hinduism, but also in the minds of the people. One reason for this
is that the Brahmans in their effort to absorb the Dravidian people and religion
have to some extent identified Dravidian demons with their own "Rakshasas".'
[2] Demons may also be 'depressed' gods.
[3] Dr. Franks, ad loc., *P. C.*, p. 348, says: 'The Satan is, like the angels in
general, a relic of a polydaemonistic stage of religion. With the disappearance
of polydaemonism before monotheism, the Satan has become a minister of the
Divine Providence. But he is still somewhat of a free lance—even Yahweh has
to ask where he has been.' I should have thought that it was at least as likely
that the Satan here is a product of the evolution of angelology. The Satan of
the N. T. is still more of a 'free lance'.
[4] I do not think it necessary to examine this.
[5] Part of the 'Holiness Code'. So Kennedy, *Cent. Bib.*, ad loc.

mythology.'   In Isa. xxxiv. 14 reference is made to the לִילִית
as well as to the שָׂעִיר. Compare the generally accepted
emendation[2] of 2 Kings xxiii. 8 b from 'He brake down the
high places of the gates (אֶת־בָּמוֹת הַשְּׁעָרִים)' to 'He brake down
the high places of the satyrs (אֶת־בָּמוֹת הַשְּׂעִירִים)'.

To return to Mr. Abrahams' argument: He seeks to
minimize the force of the evidence of Josephus in respect of
belief in demons, and, in particular, hints that the Jew Eleazar[3]
was indulging in exotic practices when he exorcized the
demon in the presence of Vespasian.   The two references to
demoniac possession in Josephus (*Wars*, vii. vi. 3; *Antiq.* viii.
ii. 5) are certainly remarkable for the magical ideas which
they exhibit, and are quite on a par with the most grossly
superstitious ideas to be found in the Babylonian Talmud.
None the less it would be hazardous to maintain that he,
a Jew of Palestine, was putting forward beliefs entirely remote
from Palestinian thought in his time (i.e. in the first century
A.D.).   In the 'general assertion' in the *Wars* he describes
the means necessary to obtaining the Baaras root, and continues : 'Yet after all this pains of getting, it is only valuable
on account of one virtue it hath, that if it be only brought to
the sick persons, it quickly drives away those called demons,
which are no other than the spirits of the wicked, that enter
into men that are alive, and kill them, unless they can obtain
some help against them.'[4]

In the account of the cure by exorcism in the 'Antiquities'
it is very significant that the story is told avowedly to magnify
Solomon.   Josephus almost apologizes for giving so much
space to these matters, but he does it that men may know 'the
vastness of Solomon's abilities'.   The mention of Vespasian
and the distinguished people about him as being present at
the cures is surely introduced by the writer to show that he is
not simply narrating some 'cock and bull' story.   It is purely
incidental that the case is 'associated with the Roman imperial
family'.[5]   It will be well to quote from the passage in question
in order to show where the real emphasis of the story lies :

---

[1] Kennedy,'Leviticus', *Cent Bib.*,p.121. Cf. Dr Buchanan Gray, *E. B.* 4301.
[2] See Skinner, *Cent. Bib* , ad loc.   This is, of course, only an emendation of
the Massoretic pointing, and does not involve an alteration of the text.
[3] *Antiq.*, viii. ii. 5.
[4] William Whiston's translation.   [5] Abrahams.

'God also enabled him (i. e. Solomon) to learn the skill which expels demons, which is a science useful and sanative to men. He composed such incantations also by which distempers are alleviated, and he left behind him the manner of using exorcisms, by which they drive away demons, so that they never return : and this method of cure is of great force unto this day : for I have seen a certain man of my own country whose name was Eleazar, releasing people that were demoniacal in the presence of Vespasian, and his sons and his captains, and the whole multitude of his soldiers. The manner of the cure was this : he put a ring that had a root of one of those sorts mentioned by Solomon to the nostrils of the demoniac, after which he drew out the demon through his nostrils : and when the man fell down immediately, he abjured him to return no more, making still mention of Solomon, and reciting the incantations which he composed. And when Eleazar would persuade and demonstrate to the spectators that he had such a power, he set a little way off a cup or bason full of water, and commanded the demon, as he went out of the man, to overturn it, and thereby to let the spectators know that he had left the man [1] : and when this was done, the skill and wisdom of Solomon was shewed very manifestly ', &c.[2]

The belief that disease was due to demonic influence was prevalent amongst the Assyrians and Babylonians. ' The whole of the cuneiform incantations are full of the belief that some god, demon, or ghost is plaguing the sick man, and must be expelled before the patient can be healed.'[3] This belief did not apply merely to the patient who was suffering from the peculiar morbid condition in which a man feels himself to be controlled by some malignant spirit not himself, but also to one who was suffering from some quite ordinary complaint such as, e.g. headache.[4] That a large section of the Jews was not immune from the infection of beliefs such as this the Babylonian Talmud is witness. The difficulty is to judge how far this was so during the period of our Lord's

---

[1] Cf. the 'Gerasene Demoniac . Also Philostratus, *Apollonius of Tyana*, Bk. IV, ch. xx, and Budge, *The Book of Syriac Medicines*, vol. ii, p. 711.
[2] Whiston.
[3] R. Campbell Thompson, art. ' Disease and Medicine ' (Assyro-Babylonian), *E. R. E.*
[4] Cf. R. C. Thompson, ibid.

ministry. The extracts given above from Josephus point to an early date when ideas of this kind began to spread. The Synoptists are in no doubt about the existence of demonic possession, and Mt. and Lk., at least, occasionally show an inclination to attribute disease in general to this cause.[1] That Mk. distinguishes clearly between demonic possession and other maladies is significant. Our evidence is somewhat conflicting, but it does not justify us in assuming that in Palestine during the first half of the first century A.D. the popular diagnosis of all disease was that it was due to demonic influence, and still less in assuming that Jesus took this view.[2] Our Lord, however, seems to have believed that there was such a thing as demon possession. Indeed it appears that He felt the casting out of demons to be a Messianic function.[3] Certainly the Synoptists thought this to be so. Harnack [4] is right when he says (speaking of the significance of exorcism for primitive Christianity) : 'One must remember that according to the belief of Christians the Son of God came into the world to combat Satan and his kingdom. The evangelists, especially Luke, have depicted the life of Jesus from the temptation onwards as an uninterrupted conflict with the devil ; what he came for was to destroy the works of the devil.' Compare, e.g. that saying of Q (Mt. xii. 28 = Lk. xi. 20) : εἰ δὲ

---

[1] c.g. Mt ix. 32-34, xii 22-24 ; Lk. xi. 14-16, viii 10-17 Minor indications of this will be pointed out below.

[2] I think Mr. H. G. Wood, *P. C.*, p. 663, is wrong on this point. Note further that ideas concerning sickness and the physician such as are found in Ecclus xxxviii no doubt formed part of the mental background during this period. There is no suggestion of demons here—though there is of sin.

[3] As is indicated below the four Gospels unite in the belief that the age is under the sway of Satan The Messiah is to destroy his rule and power Part of the work of this destruction is the overcoming of disease. Lk. x. 17-20 (peculiar to Lk.) is very instructive. The words ἐθεώρουν τὸν σαταναν ὡς ἀστραπὴν ἐκ τοῦ οὐρανοῦ πεσόντα follow immediately the account of the return of the Seventy rejoicing that καὶ τὰ δαιμόνια ὑποτάσσεται ἡμῖν ἐν τῷ ὀνόματί σου, and Jesus goes on to say that He has given them power to tread on serpents and scorpions and to trample down πᾶσαν τὴν δύναμιν τοῦ ἐχθροῦ, and that nothing shall hurt them. The outburst of praise in the following verses (21-24) from Q is very significant in this connexion. The idea of Satan as holding temporary sway over the present world is not confined to the Gospels ; it runs throughout the N. T., and is conspicuous in St. Paul. Cf., e.g. Rom. xvi 10 , 1 Cor. v. 5, vii 5 , 2 Cor. ii. 11, xi. 14 ; 1 Thess. ii. 18; also Eph. vi. 11 ; 1 Pet. v 8 ; 1 Jn. iii 8, &c.

[4] *Expansion of Christianity*, p 159.

ἐν πνεύματι (Lk. δακτύλῳ) θεοῦ ἐγὼ ἐκβάλλω τὰ δαιμόνια, ἄρα ἔφθασεν ἐφ᾽ ὑμᾶς ἡ βασιλεία τοῦ θεοῦ.[1] Notice too how Mk. brackets together preaching and casting out demons; e.g. Mk. i. 39 (. . . κηρύσσων . . . καὶ τὰ δαιμόνια ἐκβάλλων); iii. 14, 15 (καὶ ἐποίησεν δώδεκα . . . ἵνα ἀποστέλλῃ αὐτοὺς κηρύσσειν καὶ ἔχειν ἐξουσίαν ἐκβάλλειν τὰ δαιμόνια); and vi. 7, 12 and prls.[2]

The Fourth Gospel is one with the Synoptics in maintaining the belief in the conflict between Jesus and Satan and his kingdom. Compare the ὁ ἄρχων τοῦ κόσμου (τούτου) of Jn. xii. 31, xiv. 30, xvi. 11.

Summary. The evidence for a fairly widespread belief in demons in Palestine in the time of our Lord is strong. It is probable, however, that the extent of this belief varied in different localities according to the degree in which they were open to foreign influence. It is possible that Judea was comparatively immune from it, but the people there were not so isolated as to make it likely that they were unaffected by the opinions of the peoples round about them. We are unable to argue ·much from the silence of the Gospels as to demon possession in Judea. The Synoptists record only the shortest of Judean ministries, and that filled with more vital matters; while Jn., if he mentions no exorcisms in Judea, is equally silent about them in any other region.

It is not possible to say with certainty where or when this belief in demons started amongst the Jews. Probably there was no one source. Mr. Conybeare[3] says that the *locus classicus* for the origin of demons is found in Enoch xv. From it we learn that the strong or evil spirits, which have their habitation on earth, are the giants that were begotten of mortal women by the watchers of heaven, the angels. There can be no doubt that this chapter was powerful in influencing

---

[1] Moffatt, *The Theology of the Gospels*, p. 50, on this passage says: ' This . . . means that the new era has already begun to challenge and invade the present sway of the devil on earth. As the context indicates, the messianic power of Jesus on earth denotes an inroad upon the demons who, under Satan, have control of men, and this inroad is the entrance of God's kingdom upon its final career.'

[2] Cf. H. G. Wood, *P. C.*, p. 663 : 'From Mk.'s gospel it appears that the driving out of demons was an essential part of the proclamation of the Kingdom.'

[3] F. C. Conybeare, *J. Q. R.*, vol. ix, p. 75.

subsequent thought.   Delitzsch [1] suggests that demoniac
possession and exorcisms are (so far as the Jews are concerned)
of Babylonian origin, the doctrine of demons being introduced
into Jewish beliefs partly in the Exile, and partly by the
foreign colonists from Babylonian cities who were settled in
Galilee and Samaria in the eighth and seventh centuries B.C.
He says that it is a distinction of old Israelite religion that it
was free from a belief in demons.   Loisy,[2] on the other hand,
thinks that the ideas about demon possession in the time of
Jesus were influenced by the extensive development of angelology and demonology amongst the Jews after the time of the
Persian domination, but adds, ' Mais l'ensemble des croyances
populaires dont dépendent ces idées se retrouve beaucoup
plus anciennement dans la tradition d'Israël '.   I cannot help
thinking this last very probable, although there does not
seem to be much direct evidence for it.   At any rate there
are to be found in the various stages of O. T. religion beliefs
which would link themselves on without much difficulty to
foreign demonic beliefs.

Another source for the belief in demons naturally might be
the presence of lunatics wandering at large about the country-
side.   If this was the state of affairs in England at the present
day, how would it affect the opinions of the common people ?[3]

But whatever its origin or origins the belief was there—
perhaps not always clearly formulated, yet ever in the background of men's minds as a possible solution of uncanny
phenomena.   The importance of this for our purpose is that,
being there, it was liable to affect the form which diseases
(especially mental ones) would take,[4] and also to affect their
diagnosis.

[1] F. Delitzsch, *Mehr Licht*, p. 52, quoted by Montefiore, *S. G.* 1. 66.
[2] *E. S.* i. 453
[3] Cf. Dr. Headlam, *The Miracles of the New Testament*, p. 302 f.
[4] Cf. Harnack, *Expansion of Christianity*, vol. i, p. 152 f

V

LEPROSY

Introduction

WHATEVER may be the precise diagnosis of the diseases described in Lev. xiii. 1 ff. as צָרַעַת, 'leprosy', it is generally admitted that they do not include what is meant by leprosy at the present day—tubercular or anaesthetic leprosy. Indeed it has been held doubtful whether any one would ever have discovered true leprosy in these chapters in Leviticus but for the translation of צָרַעַת by λέπρα (LXX ; Vulg. *lepra*).[1] The main reasons for this may be summarized as follows [2] :

According to Leviticus the characteristic features of leprosy were : (1) bright white spots or patches on the skin, the hair on which also was white ; (2) the depression of the patches below the level of the surrounding skin ; (3) the existence of 'quick raw flesh' ; (4) the spreading of the scab or scall.

Compare this with the description of modern leprosy. I quote from Schamberg.[3] 'There are two forms of modern leprosy—the tubercular, or nodular, and the anaesthetic, or nervous ; generally both forms are present. The nodular form begins, as a rule, as round or irregularly shaped spots, commonly of a mahogany or sepia colour. These often disappear, and are followed by the appearance of nodules. In an advanced stage the face is covered with firm, livid, nodular elevations : the nose, lips, and ears are swollen beyond their natural size, the eyelashes and eyebrows are lost, and the eyes are staring ; the whole producing a hideous disfigurement. As the disease progresses, insensibility of the skin and paralysis ensue, and the fingers and toes may rot away.'[4]

[1] Creighton, art. 'Leprosy', *E. B* See also Kennedy, 'Leviticus', *Cent. Bib.*, p. 90 f.
[2] See J. F Schamberg, M.D., art. 'Leprosy', *J. E.*
[3] Op. cit.
[4] Cf. the definition of leprosy in Sir William Osler's *The Principles and Practice of Medicine* (8th ed., p 151) : 'A chronic infectious disease caused by 'Bacillus leprae', characterized by the presence of tubercular nodules in the skin and mucous membranes (tubercular leprosy) or by changes in the nerves

Note in the Biblical description the absence of allusion to
the hideous facial deformity, the loss of feeling, and the rotting
of members. Further, the Levitical regulations prescribed
that the examinations should be made at intervals of seven
days to enable the priest to note the progress of the disease.
But modern leprosy 'is an exceedingly slow disease, particularly in the beginning, and a fortnight would show absolutely
no change in the vast majority of cases'.[1] Also, provision
was made for cure in a way that does not in the least suggest
that it was exceptional, whereas modern leprosy is (so far as
our present knowledge goes) next door to incurable. The
Levitical prescriptions were not made for sanitary purposes.
Leprosy was not considered contagious in the modern sense ;
the uncleanness was a ritual uncleanness.[2] The Mishnah
does not consider a leprous pagan or unnaturalized prose-
lyte ritually unclean (Nega'im iii. 1, xi. 1). If a bridegroom
on his wedding-day observes symptoms of leprosy on his skin
he is not required to submit himself for examination at once,
but may postpone it until the seven days of his nuptials are
over. Similarly, one who is affected with it during the holy
days may postpone examination till they are over (Neg. iii. 2).[3]
Again, in the story of Abba Taḥna in Ecclesiasticus Rabba
(on ix. 7), what the poor man troubled about was that, if he
left his goods to help the leper, he would lose them, and have
nothing to sustain himself and his household. Fear of catching the disease did not come into the question.[4]

It is noteworthy that in the description of λέπρα in the
medical writings of Aegineta, Aetius, Actuarius, and others
'there is absolutely nothing . . . that suggests even in a remote
manner the modern leprosy. The Greeks, in speaking of true
leprosy, did not use the term "lepra ", but "elephantiasis ".'[5]

(anaesthetic leprosy). At first these forms may be separate, but ultimately both
are combined, and in the characteristic tubercular form there are disturbances
of sensation.' See also Latham and Torrens, *Medical Diagnosis*, p. 125 f.

   [1] Schamberg.

   [2] Cf. Kennedy, p. 91. Especially see Robertson Smith, *Rel of Sem.* (e. g.
Additional Note B, p. 446 ff.).

   [3] See A S. Waldstein, art 'Leprosy', *J. E.*

   [4] For the story see Abrahams, op. cit., ch. xiii.

   [5] Schamberg, op. cit. He thinks that λέπρα as described by them was the
modern 'psoriasis'.

It seems likely that the Hebrews attached much the same meaning to נֶגַע as the Greeks did to λέπρα, which is the word used in the LXX to translate it. A further point to be noted is that in Leviticus garments (xiii. 47–59) and houses (xiv. 33–53) are held capable of being smitten with the plague of 'leprosy.'

It is probable that 'leprosy' was used to describe not merely one disease, but a number of skin diseases [1] (and applied by analogy to garments and houses). One such disease which seems to be indicated is 'vitiligo'.[2]

From what has been said above it is clear that when we come upon λέπρα or λεπρός in the N. T. we cannot assume that the word refers to leprosy in the modern sense. It may possibly bear this meaning, but it is as likely, indeed more likely, to refer to some milder skin disease.

Mk. i. 40–45; Mt. viii. 1-4 ; Lk. v. 12–16.

 Mk. καὶ ἔρχεται πρὸς αὐτὸν λεπρός
 Mt. καὶ ἰδοὺ λεπρὸς προσελθών
 Lk καὶ ἰδοὺ ἀνὴρ πλήρης λέπρας

The Evangelists agree in main outline in their account of the incident, and agree verbally as to the method of treatment. The chief points of verbal identity to notice are that the man comes beseeching Jesus and says, ἐὰν θέλῃς δύνασαί με καθαρίσαι, and that Jesus takes up his words and says, θέλω, καθαρίσθητι, having first stretched out His hand and touched [3] him.

But from Mk. we clearly obtain the earliest and most accurate account. He gives us something of the 'atmosphere' of the incident which is lacking in Mt. and Lk. Moreover, his setting helps to make the incident more intelligible, especially in the light of the additional information which he gives. He shows us that Jesus in these early days of His

---

[1] Cf. Sir William Osler, *The Principles and Practice of Medicine*, 8th ed., p. 151 : 'The disease appears to have prevailed in Egypt even so far back as three or four thousand years before Christ. The Hebrew writers make many references to it, but, as is evident from the description in Leviticus, many forms of skin disease were embraced under the term leprosy.'

[2] So Schamberg, op. cit., and Münch, *Die Zaraath der hebr. Bibel*, pp. 110-14 (quoted Kennedy, ' Leviticus ', p. 92).

[3] Cf. Mk. i. 31, v. 23, 41, vii. 33, viii. 22 f., ix. 27.

ministry felt that preaching was His first duty (cf. i. 38 εἰς τοῦτο
γὰρ ἐξῆλθον), and how He was obstructed in His purpose by the
continual calls upon His powers of healing. These calls are
vividly portrayed in the first chapter and the beginning of the
second. This perhaps gives us a partial clue to the force of
the strong word ἐμβριμησάμενος.[1] Our Lord was too com-
passionate to resist the appeal for help, and yet He was
indignant[2] at being increasingly hindered from His proper
mission. The more He cured the more would come to be
cured. How handicapped would He be even if all the lepers
alone flocked to Him to be healed! Ver. 45 makes quite clear
the inconvenience our Lord is caused by this very act of healing.[3] The Marcan account, as we have it, makes it by no
means improbable that the reading ὀργισθείς (ver. 41) of Daff[?]
for σπλαγχνισθείς is the original reading.[4] Such a word might
well be changed from motives of reverence. Further, if
ὀργισθείς, or its Aramaic equivalent, was in the original source
employed by Mt. and Lk. we can understand why these
Evangelists have avoided any word describing our Lord's
emotions. It is to be observed that they omit the Marcan
ἐμβριμησάμενος, and also the curious phrase in this place εὐθὺς
ἐξέβαλεν αὐτόν. This last phrase suggests that the scene of
the incident was a house.[5] There seems therefore a second
explanation (not necessarily exclusive of the first) for the
atmosphere of indignation apparent in Mk.'s narrative. The
leper, unlike the ten lepers of Lk. xvii, did not 'stand afar
off' but actually came into the house where Jesus was, thus

---

[1] Hatch, *Essays in Biblical Greek*, p 25, holds that the word should be explained by its use (1) as a translation of זָעַם 'to be angry', and (2) as a translation of גָּעַר 'to rebuke'. Thus, e. g. (1) in Aquil. Ps. vii 12 ἐμβριμώμενος
(= LXX ὀργὴν ἐπάγων); (2) in Symm. Is. xvii. 13 ἐμβριμήσεται αὐτῷ (= LXX
ἀποσκορακιεῖ αὐτόν; Aquil. ἐπιτιμήσει ἐν αὐτῷ). So ἐμβρίμησις translates the
derivative גְּעָרָה in Symm. Ps. lxxv. (lxxvi.) 7 = LXX Aquil ἐπιτιμήσεως.

[2] I doubt if this word is quite right, and yet it is difficult to find a more suitable one which does sufficient justice to ἐμβριμησάμενος. But see below, p. 93,
n. 1.

[3] Lk. v 15, 16 echoes this verse, but obscures the real situation. He is
careful to avoid mention of the leper's disobedience to our Lord's command

[4] Moffatt, *I. L. N. T.*, p 233, thinks this preferable. On the other hand
Dalman, *The Words of Jesus*, p. 65, speaks of the 'unmeaning ὀργισθείς'.

[5] So H. G. Wood, *P. C*, ad loc.

flagrantly breaking the law ¹ (cf. Lev. xiii. 46). Whether our Lord objected to the man's breaking the law as such must remain doubtful, but it is, at any rate, quite clear that it was extremely embarrassing for Him at that stage in His ministry to be associated in the minds of the authorities with a breach of this kind. His forcible insistence on the man's complying with the Mosaic regulations when he is cured is thus readily intelligible.

Note the intensity of the faith which the leper must have had to take the step which he did.

Result of treatment :

Mk. εὐθὺς ἀπῆλθεν ἀπ' αὐτοῦ ἡ λέπρα, καὶ ἐκαθαρίσθη.
Mt. εὐθέως ἐκαθαρίσθη αὐτοῦ ἡ λέπρα.²
Lk. εὐθέως ἡ λέπρα ἀπῆλθεν ἀπ' αὐτοῦ.²

Summary of important points for our purpose :

Disease: some skin affection to which the Levitical law concerning 'leprosy' was applicable.
Method of cure : Jesus touches the man, and commands him authoritatively to be cleansed, employing the man's own words.
Atmosphere: intense. Jesus combines indignation with compassion.³ Great faith on the part of the patient.
Result: immediate cure.

Lk. xvii. 11-19.

ὑπήντησαν αὐτῷ δέκα λεπροὶ ἄνδρες.

The stress in the story is laid not on the healing, but on the fact that the one who returned to give thanks was a Samaritan. Lk. shows an interest in Samaria: cf. ix. 52, x. 33 ; Acts viii (all peculiar to him). It is possible that these accounts were derived from Philip the deacon, the first evangelist of Samaria.⁴ It is not reasonable to suppose that the narrative here is dependent upon that just examined above, since the details

---

¹ The breach of the law is plain even if we reject the 'house' theory.
² An interesting example of the way in which Mt. sometimes borrows one half and Lk. the other of a statement by Mk. Cf. Mt viii. 16 = Mk. i. 32 = Lk. iv. 40.
³ The compassion is evident whether we read σπλαγχνισθείς or not.
⁴ So J. M. Thompson, *M. N. T.*, p. 89. See Acts xxi. 8.

are entirely different (with the exception of the order πορευ-
θέντες ἐπιδείξατε ἑαυτοὺς τοῖς ἱερεῦσιν, which may possibly be an
echo of Mk. i. 44. prls.). Cf. the message to John in Q, Mt.
xi. 5 = Lk. vii. 22 : λεπροὶ καθαρίζονται : also Mt. x. 8 and Lk.
iv. 27. The setting of the story is somewhat vague (cf. e g
the τινα κώμην of ver. 12).[1] As it stands the salient points for
us are :

(1) The men, conforming with the law, ἔστησαν πόρρωθεν.

(2) From this distance they call out, Ἰησοῦ ἐπιστάτα, ἐλέησον
ἡμᾶς.

(3) When Jesus notices them, all He does is to tell them to
go and show themselves to the priests, i.e. in a very subtle
way He suggests to them that they are already healed.[2]

(4) They depart, and discover on the way that they are
cleansed (cf. vv. 14 and 15).[3]

(5) One, a Samaritan described as ἀλλογενής, returns to give
Jesus thanks, and Jesus says to him ἡ πίστις σου σέσωκέν σε.

We have seen that 'leprosy' in the N. T. is a term that
may have been used to cover almost any kind of skin disease.
Clearly, therefore, it is not possible to bring forward modern
instances with any certainty that they bear any resemblance
to the cases recorded in the Gospels. The most we can do
is to show that various forms of skin disease have proved
amenable to mental treatment.

Instances of severe cases of warts being cured by suggestion
alone have already been indicated.[4] Treatment in a similar
way of eczema and like affections has also been successful.
I quote two examples of the influence of the mind in such
cases from Dr. J. Bonjour: 'Moi-même, j'ai été le témoin de

[1] It is not necessary for the purpose in hand to go into the interesting ques-
tions arising out of ver. 11. See Moffatt, *I. L. N. T*, p. 452, Burkitt, *The
Gospel History and its Transmission*, p. 96 f., Streeter, *O. S. S. P.*, p. 159,
J. M. Thompson, op. cit, p. 88 f.

[2] Cf. the story of Elisha and Naaman (scene also Samaria) in 2 Kings v.
The parallel is not, however, complete.

[3] It is futile to discuss whether really only one of them was cured. The
evidence is perhaps a trifle stronger for the tenth than for the other nine. On
the other hand the cure of one would increase the likelihood of the cure of
others. The whole evidence is too doubtful to allow of judgement on the
matter.

[4] See above, p. 111

guérisons instantanées de maladies organiques et microbiennes à la suite d'une émotion. Un malade atteint d'eczéma prurigineux, devenu secondairement le siège de lésions microbiennes, a guéri en 48 heures après une émotion, alors que la maladie avait résisté aux soins éclairés des professeurs Lassar, de Berlin, Fournier, de Paris, et Kaposy, de Vienne. Une malade a guéri en quelques heures d'une affection pityriasique de la peau s'étendant du cou aux pieds. Cette malade a été examinée et suivie par un spécialiste auquel je l'avais adressée. Il fit d'abord le diagnostic d'eczéma, puis de pityriasis. L'affection cutanée disparut en une nuit à la suite d'une émotion que je provoquai afin que la malade se soumit aux exigences que nécessitait le traitement.'[1] Bonjour holds that a state of light hypnosis ('Hypnose, 1er degré') is sufficient in order to cure eczema by suggestion.[2]

Prof. Baudouin records the case of a woman of Nancy who had suffered for three years from 'an intractable eczema of the hands', who was cured by suggestion in a few sittings in 1914.[3]

Apart from specific examples, even the little knowledge we have of the powers of suggestion would lead us to believe that many skin diseases could be at least mitigated by this agency. We have seen that suggestion is capable of influencing the blood-supply and also of abolishing pain.[4] If Dr. Hadfield's experiments (referred to on p. 12 ff.) point in the right direction, the removal of pain tends to accelerate the healing process. Supposing, therefore, a man suffering from a disease of the skin accepts the suggestion of a healer that he is cured, he will (if he has really accepted the suggestion) cease to feel pain or irritation in the affected part. Moreover, since he believes himself to be cured, his unconscious will probably automatically regulate the blood-supply to the diseased area in the most favourable way possible.[5]

---

[1] *Les Guérisons miraculeuses modernes*, p. 15 f.

[2] Vide ibid., p. 45.

[3] See *Suggestion and Autosuggestion*, p. 234   The case was recorded in the *Bulletin École de Nancy*, 1914.

[4] See p. 13 above.

[5] This statement is not arbitrary. It seems that the unconscious often will work out in detail the implications of a very general suggestion. Cf. Baudouin, op. cit, p. 156 f.

Thus two powerful factors will be at work to bring about the actual cure which the patient believes already to have taken place.

It is evident that certain skin diseases at least do not need to be hysterical in origin (in the sense of being caused by suggestion) in order that they may be amenable to treatment by psychotherapy.

VI

DEMON POSSESSION

A. *Introduction, &c.*

THE term ' demon possession ' covers a fairly definite group of symptoms. As indicated above Mk. differentiates it clearly from other ailments. It is probably true to say that no modern Christian missionary who has come into vital contact with people of primitive culture and religion would be in any doubt as to its distinctive character. A definition of the malady is scarcely possible ; it will be sufficient to point out its main distinguishing feature. This is best put in the words of Loisy : ' Le caractère pathologique de la possession consiste dans l'éclipse totale ou partielle, continue ou intermittente, de la personnalité.' [1]

In this section, therefore, I shall follow the indications of Mk., and not include Mt. ix. 32-34 (dumb demoniac), Mt. xii. 22-24 = Lk. xi. 14-16 (dumb [and blind] demoniac), or Lk. xiii. 10-17 (woman with spirit of infirmity).[2]

The modern mission-field has light to give us for the interpretation of the N. T. demon possession narratives. Some of the evidence which it affords will be adduced in the next section.

---

[1] *E. S* i. 452. He continues with a more particular diagnosis.
[2] For these see below.

Mk. i. 23-28 ; Lk. iv. 33-37.

Mk. ἄνθρωπος ἐν πνεύματι ἀκαθάρτῳ [1]
Lk. ἄνθρωπος ἔχων πνεῦμα δαιμονίου ἀκαθάρτου

In the Evangelists' picture of this scene in the synagogue at Capernaum the chief emphasis is laid upon the manifestation by Jesus of ἐξουσία in word and deed. We may see here an underlying didactic purpose, but that is not to say that the incident is unhistorical. Indeed the whole account of this Sabbath day together with that of the healing of the crowds immediately the Sabbath was over rings thoroughly true. If the setting (to say nothing of the incidents) is purely fictitious the original author must have been a singularly penetrating psychologist. The whole of the section Mk. i. 21-34 and prls. hangs together, each part being made more intelligible by that which has preceded it.

Lk. agrees with Mk. in main outline, and to some extent verbally. The verbal differences are, however, considerable, but I doubt if they are of a kind to make probable a separate or corroborating source. The incident with which we are dealing belongs undoubtedly to an early stage in our Lord's ministry. Apart from other considerations, the fact that He is teaching and healing in a synagogue is witness to this.

Behaviour of the man : He shrieks at Jesus in opposition and terror : τί ἡμῖν καὶ σοί,[2] Ἰησοῦ Ναζαρηνέ ; ἦλθες ἀπολέσαι ἡμᾶς ;[3] οἴδαμέν σε τίς εἶ, ὁ ἅγιος τοῦ θεοῦ.[4]

N.B.—the reference to himself in the plural. It is not quite clear whether 'us' is meant to refer to the man + the demon or to a plurality of demons. Verses 23 and 25 prls obviously suggest the former, but the ἦλθες ἀπολέσαι ἡμᾶς of ver. 24 prl. is more doubtful. These words seem to have reference to the current beliefs concerning the fate of demons in the 'Age

---

[1] Cf. Mk. xii. 36 ἐν τῷ πνεύματι τῷ ἁγίῳ. The expressions are parallel ; but although the language and thought of the time spoke of 'unclean spirits' it never spoke of 'holy spirits'.

[2] Cf. below, p. 56, n. 1.

[3] Perh. interrog. But this punctuation (Huck, *Synopse*) for the Marcan version seems more effective, and is psychologically much more likely.

[4] What have we to do with thee, Jesus of Nazareth ? Thou art come to destroy us We know who thou art—the Holy One of God.

to Come'.[1] If this is so it is scarcely likely that the man would couple himself with the demon in sharing the expectation of a common fate. Rather we should take 'us' to indicate 'demons'. As we shall see, I think, when we come to consider the incident in the light of psychological research the confusion here apparent is natural enough not only in the reporters but also in the consciousness of the patient himself. Loisy [2] puts the position succinctly and reasonably : ' comme il s'identifie au démon qui est en lui il parle pour cet esprit et pour tous les démons.' In a similar way the οἶδα of Lk. is quite as likely as the οἴδαμεν [3] of Mk.

The demoniac recognizes Jesus as Messiah—ὁ ἅγιος τοῦ θεοῦ.[4] Lk. may be held to be a trifle more dramatic than Mk. in his description—e. g. φωνῇ μεγάλῃ and the interjection ἔα. But the phrase φωνῇ μεγάλῃ,[5] at least, is rather redundant with a word like ἀνακράζω.

Method of treatment: wholly verbal. Our Lord is stern. ἐπετίμησεν αὐτῷ, saying, φιμώθητι καὶ ἔξελθε ἐξ (Lk. ἀπ') αὐτοῦ.

Result : According to Mk. the unclean spirit came out of the man after having convulsed him (σπαράξαν αὐτόν) and given vent to a loud cry (φωνῆσαν φωνῇ μεγάλῃ).

According to Lk. the demon flung the man down in

---

[1] Cf. the more def. reference in Mt. viii. 29 ἦλθες ὧδε πρὸ καιροῦ βασανίσαι ἡμᾶς; see Enoch, chs. vi–xix, and Jubilees, chs iv–v. Note, e. g. Enoch xix. 1, '. . . till the day of the great judgement in which they shall be judged till they are made an end of' (Charles's trans , *Pseudepigrapha of the O T.*). On the whole subject see Kirsopp Lake, *The Earlier Epistles of St. Paul*, 2nd ed., p 193 f., and F. C. Conybeare, *J. Q. R.*, vol. ix, p. 75. On the ' Age to Come ' see Foakes Jackson and Lake, *B. Chr.*, Pt. I, vol. 1, pp. 272–83

[2] *E. S.* i. 449.

[3] This is not a universal reading.

[4] Cf. Jn. vi. 69 ἡμεῖς πεπιστεύκαμεν καὶ ἐγνώκαμεν ὅτι σὺ εἶ ὁ ἅγιος τοῦ θεοῦ : Lk. i 35 Πνεῦμα ἅγιον ἐπελεύσεται ἐπὶ σέ, καὶ δύναμις Ὑψίστου ἐπισκιάσει σοι· διὸ καὶ τὸ γεννώμενον ἅγιον κληθήσεται, υἱὸς θεοῦ. Also Acts iii. 14 ; Jn. ii. 20 , Rev. iii. 7. In view of this expression and the emphasis noted above on ἐξουσία see the 17th Ps. of Solomon.

[5] Possibly the transposition of this from the Marcan position was made from motives of reverence, i. e. Lk. will not admit that the demon disobeyed the injunction to silence. Cf. above, p. 46, n. 3, on Lk. v. 15, 16. Sir John Hawkins, *Horae Synopticae*, thinks that such transpositions point to oral tradition.

front of the people (ῥῖψαν αὐτὸν εἰς τὸ μέσον) and came
out of him, doing him no injury (μηδὲν βλάψαν αὐτόν).
These two accounts differ in expression and as to details, but
they do not mutually conflict. The main symptom accompanying the cure is clear, and that is that the man fell down
in a convulsion.[1] Of Lk.'s use here of βλάπτειν Hobart[2]
says that he is writing 'quite in the manner and style of the
medical authors', and that he is indicating that 'no permanent
bodily injury was done to the man'. Mk.'s mention of the
loud cry is likely enough to be genuine and in the right
position.[3]

Mk. v. 1-20; Lk. viii. 26-39; Mt. viii. 28-34.

Mk. ἄνθρωπος ἐν πνεύματι ἀκαθάρτῳ
Lk. ἀνήρ τις . . . ἔχων δαιμόνια
Mt. δύο δαιμονιζόμενοι

In order to diagnose as far as possible this case we shall be
on firm ground (or rather, the firmest available ground) if we
follow Mk. The gist of Lk.'s account differs in no important
particular from that of Mk., and the verbal agreements
between them are considerable. Indeed Lk. does not supply
us with any new information,[4] although he brings into
prominence details which are only latent in Mk.'s story.
Thus, e. g. he tells us that the man went naked (interesting
from a diagnostic point of view), but this might reasonably

---

[1] Souter, in his *Pocket Lexicon to the Greek N. T.*, gives as the sole meaning
of σπαράσσω, 'I throw' on the ground, but it obviously has here in addition
something of its classical signification of 'tearing' or 'rending'. Moffatt
translates 'convulse' in his *New Trans. of the N. T.* Hobart, op. cit., p. 2,
shows that ῥίπτειν was used in medical language of convulsive fits and similar
affections.

[2] Op. cit., p. 2.

[3] Menzies Alexander's diagnosis, op. cit., p. 67 f., is rather too facile:
'Restricting attention to the physical symptoms here present, 3 things emerge:
(1) a loud cry; (2) a falling down; (3) a severe convulsion. But these are the
specific features of an epileptic attack, and are to be placed alongside of those
features which point to acute insanity. By correlating these two groups of
symptoms with each other the final diagnosis is reached without difficulty. The
case is one of epileptic insanity.'

[4] Cf. J. M. Thompson, op. cit., p. 85. Mr. Thompson also indicates
several small touches in Lk. in this story which bring out Jesus's power. It
does not seem to me that here Lk. adds much to Mk.

be inferred from Mk. v. 15, and does not necessarily imply special information. It is true that it is not impossible that he is employing a source or sources other than Mk., but the evidence does not admit of our assuming this. Upon Mt.'s account we can put but little reliance. It is very abbreviated, and gives us two demoniacs instead of one. Since these two unfortunates have no single characteristic by which we may distinguish between them we may allow ourselves to be sceptical about their separate identity. The most probable hypothesis is that Mt. has 'conflated' this demoniac with the one already described in the synagogue at Capernaum, just as he has provided two blind men in Mt. xx. 30 after having omitted the blind man of Mk. viii. 22-26.

The identity of the locality in which the incident took place has evidently been a puzzle from the earliest days.[1] There is a village called Khersa a little north of the centre of the eastern shore of the Sea of Galilee whose position answers well to the conditions described in Mk. and Lk. The most plausible conjecture is that Mk.'s 'Gerasa' was the Greek rendering of this name.[2] The confusion probably arose from the fact that this village was insignificant and little known, and Gerasa was taken to be the well-known town of that name in Peraea, which is obviously unsuited to the story. Mt.'s 'Gadara', a town about seven miles south-east of the Lake, is likely to be a conjecture resulting from the difficulties caused by supposing 'Gerasa' to refer to the town in Peraea. It is noteworthy that Mt. has tried to accommodate his version of the story so as to make Gadara reasonable in the circumstances (see viii. 30).[3]

Behaviour of the man: (1) He lived among the tombs. This is one of the many touches in the story which bring us into contact with folk-lore.[4] It is often almost taken for

---

[1] Witness the variety of MSS. readings

[2] See Wright, *Synopsis*, in loc.

[3] The argument is not seriously affected if we take Γεργεσηνός to have been the word originally employed by Mk., since 'Gergesa' is about as likely as 'Gerasa' as a rendering of Khersa. But if this is so it is not quite so simple to account for the confusion which arose. Souter, *Pock. Lex.*, thinks it best to regard Γερασηνός as a by-form of Γεργεσηνός, Γαδαρηνός being a conscious alteration.

[4] Cf. Loewe, *E. R. E.*, art. 'Demons and Spirits' (Jewish), and see Isa. lxv. 4.

granted that this large folk-lore element is a sign that the narrative has wandered a long way from historical accuracy.[1] But surely, in a case such as this, such elements impart, on the contrary, considerable verisimilitude to the story.

(2) He showed abnormal strength—so great that when men had bound him he succeeded in freeing himself by snapping the chains and breaking the fetters (πολλάκις πέδαις καὶ ἁλύσεσιν δεδέσθαι, καὶ διεσπάσθαι ὑπ' αὐτοῦ τὰς ἁλύσεις καὶ τὰς πέδας συντετρῖφθαι), and nobody could tame him.[2]

(3) Day and night among the tombs and hills he went about shrieking and gashing himself with stones.

(4) ? He wore no clothing.[3]

Man's behaviour in presence of Jesus, and mode of exorcism : The account is by no means clear. It looks at first sight as though Mk. v. 8 were a note added by an editor, but the two facts that the command is put in oratio recta and that Lk. follows Mk. in a similar explanatory parenthesis show that this is extremely improbable. Hence we must assume that our Lord ordered the demon to come out in the first instance unsuccessfully. This is the obvious inference from the text as it stands, and, if it is correct, the whole narrative throws a remarkably interesting light on our Lord's method. The scene would then be something as follows: The demoniac

---

[1] e. g. Montefiore, *S. G.*, vol. i, p. 138, says of this man : ' He is represented as dwelling among the tombs, inasmuch as he avoids all human intercourse, and partly because the popular belief was that demons like to haunt cemeteries.' It is not mentioned that this frequenting of tombs by madmen was an observed fact among the ancients. See *Actius de Melancholia ex Galeno, Rufo, &c.*, ch. i (Galen, xix. 702) : οἱ πλείους μέντοι ἐν σκοτεινοῖς τόποις χαίρουσι διατρίβειν καὶ ἐν μνημείοις καὶ ἐν ἐρήμοις. (Quoted by Hobart, op. cit., p. 14)

[2] Lk. summarizes these details in parenthesis. It is interesting to note in his version the way in which the fact is stressed that these symptoms were diabolical. This is one of the many instances we shall meet where Lk., in spite of h s supposed use of technical medical terms, exhibits a very different mental outlook from the scientific medical writers such as Hippocrates or Galen. Note the meaning which J. H. Moulton, *Grammar of N. T. Greek*, Prolegomena, p. 113, gives to πολλοῖς γὰρ χρόνοις συνηρπάκει αὐτόν, viz. ' it had long ago obtained and now kept complete mastery of him'. (See also ibid , p. 75.)

[3] This detail is probable enough ; it is a very common phenomenon in certain forms of insanity. Hobart, op. cit., p. 14, points out that Aretaeus notes the propensity to do this in his chapter on Mania. *Sign Morb. Diuturn.* 37 : περὶ Μανίης—ἐσθ' ὅτε ἐσθῆτάς τε ἐρρήξαντο. Mr. Campbell Thompson, *A Pilgrim's Scrip*, p. 25, corroborates a seventeenth-century writer who noted this as a frequent characteristic of madmen round about Mosul.

caught sight of Jesus from a distance, ran to Him, and (awed
by His personality) knelt before Him, shrieking aloud τί ἐμοὶ
καὶ σοί,[1] Ἰησοῦ, υἱὲ τοῦ θεοῦ τοῦ ὑψίστου;[2] Jesus, seeing the condition the man was in, immediately commanded the foul
spirit to come out of him ; whereupon the man (speaking now
in the name of, and for, the demon)[3] besought him piteously
not to torture him (ὥρκιζω σε τὸν θεόν, μή με βασανίσῃς). Our
Lord with keen insight saw that the case needed very careful
handling, and so slightly changed His tactics by attempting
to gain His purpose by employing a more conventional
method of procedure. He therefore asked for the demon's
name.[4] The reply given was λεγιὼν ὄνομά μοι, ὅτι πολλοί ἐσμεν.
Once the name was disclosed the 'game was up', and the
only thing for Legion to do was to obtain the most favourable
terms possible before departing. So they earnestly entreated
that they might not be sent out of the country.[5] Noticing

---

[1] Bergner thinks that this is an example of what the psycho analysts call
'transference' (*Quelques Traits*, &c , p. 123)

[2] Wellhausen, *Das Evang Marci*, p. 41, maintains that ὕψιστος was particularly a Gentile title for God, and thinks we can take it that the possessed was
a Gentile. He adds somewhat drolly, 'Aber den Ruf stösst gar nicht der
be-essene Mensch aus, sondern der Damon, der weder Jude noch Heide ist '.
H. A A Kennedy, *St. Paul and the Mystery-Religions*, p. 58 n., says that θεὸς
ὕψιστος was the typical title of the God of Israel in Asia Minor, the votaries of
whom had not been Jews, and yet were organized in associations apparently
only semi-pagan See also Dalman, op cit., p. 198 f. The use of this title here
together with the unusual injunction (Mk. v. 19) to the patient to go and
report what had been done to him make it exceedingly probable that the
demoniac was not a Jew. With regard to the sequence of events cf. N.
Micklem, *The Galilean*, p 37, n. 1: 'It is a mistake to suppose that the patient
immediately recognised Jesus as "Son of God Most High". It is apparent
from Mk. v. 8 that he only said this because Jesus "was saying", i e was
saying repeatedly to the demon, "Come out". Presumably the man learnt
Jesus' name either from Jesus himself or from the crowd.'

[3] N.B. the confusion between the possessed and the possessing spirit and
spirits similar to (only rather more complicated than) that noticed in the
previous case.

[4] Loisy, *E. S* i 806 : 'Selon l'opinion populaire la connaissance du nom
important à l'efficacité de la conjuration ' For evidence of this see, e. g.
Sir J G Frazer, *The Golden Bough*, 3rd ed , vol. iii, p 331 ; R. C. Thompson,
E. K. E., art ' Disease and Medicine ' (Assy o-Babylonian). Cf. Gen. xxxii.
29, Elmore, *Dravidian Gods in Modern Hinduism*, p 52 ; Joh. Warneck,
The Living Forces of the Gospel, p. 46

[5] The context suggests that the important thing for the well-being of the
demons was that they should not have to leave the tombs and haunts congenial
to them. Lk.'s ' into the abyss ' connects the request with folk-beliefs concerning the fate of demons.

a large herd of pigs grazing near by they begged that they might be sent into them. Jesus gave them leave, whereupon they left the man and apparently entered into the pigs, for the herd rushed down the cliff into the sea and were drowned.[1]

In some such way must we read the story if we agree to accept our data at all.

The rest of the account does not concern us apart from the fact that when a crowd gathered, owing to the spreading abroad of a rumour of the strange happenings, the people found to their frightened astonishment the (well-known) demoniac sitting down clothed and sane-minded.

Mk. vii. 24-30 ; Mt. xv. 21-28.

Mk. γυνὴ . . . ἧς εἶχεν τὸ θυγάτριον αὐτῆς πνεῦμα ἀκάθαρτον
Mt. ἡ θυγάτηρ μου κακῶς δαιμονίζεται

This interesting story unfortunately does not supply us with much data to go upon. Mk. evidently gives the more primitive account.[2]

The following points are relevant to our subject:

(1) The patient was thought to be afflicted by a demon (but we are not told what form the complaint took).

(2) Jesus was reluctant to accede to the woman's request because she was a foreigner.

---

[1] Cf. the Assyrian practice described by R. C. Thompson, *E. R. E*, art. 'Disease and Medicine' (Ass.-Bab.) : 'One of the commonest methods of treatment for exorcizing demons was an " atonement ". The idea in the Assyrian method is that the demon causing the sickness is to be offered a substitute for his victim, and hence a young pig or kid is taken, slaughtered, and placed near the patient. The devil goes forth at the physician's exorcism and takes up its abode in the carcass of the substitute, which can then be made away with, and the baneful influence destroyed.' For the objective demonstration of the departure of the demon cf. the passage from Josephus, *Antiq.* VIII. II. 5, quoted above, p. 39, and my note 1 ibid. In the present instance we may reasonably suppose that the process of cure involved a crisis in which the patient was violently convulsed as was the case with the Capernaum demoniac (Mk. I. 26) and with the 'epileptic boy' (Mk. ix. 26). This would seem a sufficient explanation of the stampede of the swine.

[2] N.B. the way in which the 'very untheological' διὰ τοῦτον τὸν λόγον ὕπαγε of Mk. is changed in Mt., and the conventional Matthaean formulae υἱὸς Δαυείδ (cf. Mt. ix. 27, xii. 13, xx. 30, 31, xxi. 9, 15) and ἀπὸ τῆς ὥρας ἐκείνης (cf. Mt viii. 13, ix. 22, xvii. 18). It looks somewhat as though Mt. is using a second source in this story.

(3) The woman was extremely persistent (thereby showing great faith in the powers of Jesus).

(4) He at length gives way not only (as Mt. says) because of her great faith, but also because He is delighted with her ready wit.[1]

(5) All we know of the method of cure is that Jesus stated that the demon had departed.

(6) When the woman reached home she found the child lying in bed and the demon gone.

(7) The patient was not in sight of the healer when she was cured.

An 'epileptic' boy.

Mk. ix. 14-29; Lk. ix. 37-43 a; Mt. xvii. 14-21.

This case has been generally taken to be one of epilepsy, no doubt partly because of the various symptoms described by the three Synoptists, and partly because of the expression ὅτι σεληνιάζεται[2] in Mt. xvii. 15. But we are justified in treating it in this section on 'demon possession' since Mk., who gives by far the most detailed account and the one which we shall do well to follow, describes it in terms of 'possession', and also since the details (both in Mk. and the other two Synoptists) clearly show it to belong to this group. The discussion below[3] will. I believe, make this evident. We may further note that it is extremely difficult even for very skilful physicians to diagnose true epilepsy with certainty, and to be sure that any given case is not really one of hysteria.[4] Dr. C. G. Jung says that the relationship is very close in the pictures presented by hysteria and epilepsy.

---

[1] Perhaps this does not necessarily follow from the text. The cure may have been performed previously when the woman first made her request, and unbeknown by her, Jesus keeping her in conversation because He was interested in her and enjoyed her repartee.

[2] 'The σεληνιαζόμενοι are the *epileptic*. The evidence on this point is unimpeachable. Aretaeus, in his treatise on "Chronic Diseases" (Bk. I. iv), remarks that epilepsy is regarded as a disgraceful disease; for it is supposed to be inflicted on persons who have sinned against the *moon*. Galen in his work on "Critical Days" says that the *moon* governs the period of epileptic seizures,' &c. (W. Menzies Alexander, *Demonic Possession in the N. T.*, p. 63).

[3] pp. 71-80.

[4] See Dr. R. G. Gordon, *S. H. N. S.*, vol. i, No. 3, pp. 159-66

'Recently', he continues, 'the view has even been maintained that there is no clean-cut frontier between epilepsy and hysteria, and that a difference is only to be noted in extreme cases.'[1] He quotes Steffens (*Arch. f. Psych.* xxxiii, p. 928), who says, ' We are forced to the conclusion that in essence hysteria and epilepsy are not fundamentally different, that the cause of the disease is the same, but is manifest in a diverse form, in different intensity and permanence '.

Although Mk. gives the most detailed account of the incident, his narrative is not without certain obscurities. For example, there is some confusion between the disciples, the scribes, and the crowd; also, in ver. 15 we read that the crowd on catching sight of Jesus were astonished and ran to greet Him, while in ver. 25 Jesus is described as (hastily) exorcizing the spirit because He saw the crowd (which one had understood to be already present) hastening up. Again, in ver. 17 the spirit is described as πνεῦμα ἄλαλον : in ver. 25 Jesus addresses it as τὸ ἄλαλον καὶ κωφὸν πνεῦμα.

Ver. 15 is in itself a difficulty. Some commentators have thought that it is based on Exod. xxxiv. 30, but Lagrange[2] is, I think, right in holding that it is absurd to suppose that a passage which says καὶ προστρέχοντες ἠσπάζοντο αὐτόν is adapted from one (LXX) which runs καὶ ἐφοβήθησαν ἐγγίσαι αὐτῷ (Heb. וַיִּירְאוּ מִגֶּשֶׁת אֵלָיו). He is not, however, so clearly right when he sums up its meaning by saying, ' Il y a donc simplement dans la foule une vive surprise, parce qu'on n'attendait pas Jésus '. The word ἐξεθαμβήθησαν seems to express something more than this.

Lk. (also Mt.) has omitted all the passages in which these difficulties occur. Likely enough he did this intentionally, seeing their awkwardness. But there is little doubt that the story as related by Lk. and by Mt. is based on the Marcan account. From the latter, then, we must obtain what data we can for understanding the case, even though it is not possible to give an adequate explanation of the small obscurities in it. There is nothing in the details of the disease to cause us surprise.

The symptoms to note are : That when a ' fit ' came upon him he behaved as though possessed by a demon : sometimes

[1] *Analytical Psychology*, p. 1 f.   [2] *Saint Marc*, ad loc.

the demon would throw him into the fire or into water; sometimes it would throw him to the ground, and he would foam at the mouth and grind his teeth. The result of his affliction was that he had become emaciated (ξηραίνεται). When he was brought to Jesus he fell on the ground and rolled about, foaming at the mouth. The possessing demon was described as dumb (? and deaf).

Treatment: Jesus inquires about the boy's condition from the father. With solemn adjuration He orders the demon out of the boy and forbids it to return. The result was that, after shrieking and being violently convulsed, the patient became like a corpse, and the onlookers thought he was dead. Thereupon Jesus took him by the hand and raised him, and he stood up.[1]

Note our Lord's emphasis on faith, its necessity (19), its power (23), and on prayer (? and fasting) (29).[2]

Cf. this case with Janet's 'Achille', quoted below.[3]

St. Paul cures a slave-girl in Macedonia by exorcism.

Acts xvi. 16-18.

The evidential value of this narrative is of a fairly high order since at any rate most of it forms part of a 'we-passage'. We cannot, however, be sure that the writer was actually present at the exorcism itself, recorded in ver. 18.

Ἐγένετο δὲ πορευομένων ἡμῶν εἰς τὴν προσευχήν, παιδίσκην τινὰ ἔχουσαν πνεῦμα πύθωνα [4] ὑπαντῆσαι ἡμῖν.

The girl brought much profit to her owners by fortune-telling. For a number of days she followed Paul and his party shrieking (ἔκραζεν λέγουσα), Οὗτοι οἱ ἄνθρωποι δοῦλοι τοῦ θεοῦ τοῦ ὑψίστου εἰσίν, οἵτινες καταγγέλλουσιν ὑμῖν ὁδὸν σωτηρίας.[5] Paul, apparently in an annoyed frame of mind (διαπονηθείς),

---

[1] Cf. Mk. i. 31, v. 41, 42.

[2] With respect to prayer cf. Mk. i. 35, taking into account its context.

[3] p. 74 ff.

[4] Lit. 'a spirit, a Python'. Pytho was an ancient title for the prophetess of Apollo Pythius, the slayer of the serpent Python. 'Python' thus came to mean a person possessed by a spirit of divination, and is sometimes used for a ventriloquist. (Dr. J. Vernon Bartlet, *Cent. Bib.*, ad loc.)

[5] i. e. says the late Prof. Allan Menzies, 'she . . gives her version, to be taken as inspired, of what they are'. (*P. C.*, ad loc.)

performed the exorcism with firmness : Παραγγέλλω σοι ἐν ὀνόματι Ἰησοῦ Χριστοῦ ἐξελθεῖν ἀπ᾿ αὐτῆς.[1] The cure was immediate.

When we are considering the problems raised by the
accounts of the exorcism of demons it is well to remember
that the N. T. admits that a non-disciple could and did
perform this work, although such a one is only recorded as
being successful when 'the name of' Jesus is employed.   See
Mk. ix. 38-41 = Lk. ix. 49-50 ; Mt. vii. 22. Cf. Origen,
Cels i. 6, ii. 49, where he allows that sometimes the name of
Jesus, uttered by 'unworthy (φαύλων)' exorcists, has had the
power to exorcize.[2] (But contrast Acts xix. 13-16, where
the seven sons of Sceva are described as using the name with
dire results.)

B. *Evidence from the modern Mission-field.*

In this section, in order to be brief, I can only draw upon
a very small part of the available material.   I therefore propose to deal with a small portion of the evidence from China,
the Battak tribes of Sumatra, and India.   For this purpose
my chief sources are J. L. Nevius, *Demon Possession and
Allied Themes*, and Miss Mildred Cable,[3] *The Fulfilment of
a Dream*, for China ; Joh. Warneck, *The Living Forces of
the Gospel*,[4] for the Battaks ; and W. T. Elmore, *Dravidian
Gods in Modern Hinduism*,[5] for India.[6]

As has already been said, it would be fairly generally
admitted by those competent to speak on the subject that
demon possession has certain characteristics which distinguish

---

[1] Note the use of the formula. Cf. Lk. x. 17 , Mk. xvi. 17; Mk. ix. 38-
41 = Lk. ix. 49-50 ; Mt. vii. 22, &c.
[2] See Abbott, *The Fourfold Gospel*, Sect. III, p. 167, n 1.
[3] Miss Cable is a missionary of the 'China Inland Mission'. Her chapter
on demonology shows careful study and observation. It is difficult, after reading the book, to doubt the substantial accuracy of her facts, even though she
may show a slight and natural bias in her interpretation of them.
[4] E. T. by Neil Buchanan (1909). The first 130 pages are devoted to a
detailed examination of the beliefs and practices of animistic heathenism.
[5] Reprinted from the *University Studies of the University of Nebraska*,
vol. xv, No 1, 1915
[6] In subsequent notes in this section I shall use the letters N, C, W, and E
respectively to refer to the above-mentioned books.

it from other complaints. It is important not to ignore the
fact that sober-minded observers find it hard to avoid the
conclusion that the term demon possession is an accurate
description of the malady. Also, the peoples amongst whom
the phenomena occur are in no sort of doubt that demon
possession differs from other diseases, and that demon
possession is demon possession. Amongst them the thought
in this respect is exactly parallel to that which we find in
the N. T. While there may be some haziness as to whether
ordinary diseases are attributable to natural causes or demonic
(and, indeed, some are definitely attributed to demonic) there
is no question that these differ from 'demonic possession'
proper. Thus Nevius says, 'The Chinese of the present day
[i. e. circ. 1897] have separate and distinct names for idiocy,
insanity, epilepsy, and hysteria, which they ascribe to physical
derangement as their immediate cause, regarding them as
quite distinct from demon possession. They not unfrequently
ascribe diseases of various kinds to evil spirits, as their
originating causes, considering them, however, as differing
from the same diseases originating without the agency of
spirits only in origin and not in nature, and as quite distinct
from the abnormal conditions of "possession".'[1] A similar
clear distinction is made by the Battak tribes.[2]

On the other hand it is necessary to bear in mind that the
phenomena of possession are frequent in societies where
there is a widespread belief in the existence of spirits and
demons, and are extremely rare (if they occur at all) where
such beliefs are not effectively held. Consequently we find
them in localities where the religion of the people is in the
main animistic, and but rarely where the general culture is on
a higher level[3] Possession in Western Europe is not
common, although, as will be seen in a later section, pathological cases are occasionally met with in which phenomena
are exhibited which can be scarcely distinguished from, if
they are not identical with, those characteristic of this malady.
It is significant that even in countries where possession is
well known cases are more common in remote parts of the
country than in cities where there is more contact with the

---

[1] N, p. 180   [2] W, p 73.
[3] Cf Harnack, *The Expansion of Christianity.* p 152 f., also E, p 51, n. 1.

outside world.[1] A Chinese of Pekin wrote in reply to a questionary sent out by Nevius, 'Cases of possession are less frequent in peaceful times, and more frequent in times of civil commotion ; less frequent in prosperous families, more so in unlucky ones ; less frequent among educated people, and more so among the ignorant'.[2] Warneck, writing of the Battaks, remarks that ' possession rarely comes to a man unprepared, and at a time when no one is thinking of it '.[3]

We may distinguish two forms of possession : (1) voluntary possession, and (2) involuntary possession. The former exhibits phenomena such as we associate with the medium at a spiritualistic séance, the latter is markedly similar to the descriptions of possession in the Gospels. But the distinction is not a hard and fast one, and examples from both groups often display important characteristics in common.

The following is an example of class (1) from Warneck [4] :—

'The soul of the dead may . . . settle on a living man as a medium (Shamanism) . . . According to reliable statements of intelligent Battak Christians who were eye and ear witnesses and partly media themselves, such an event is enacted as follows. The relatives or families of the tribe are gathered together on the village street, preferably at night, in order to consult the ancestor. The drums begin to beat their muffled monotone.[5] The medium, man or woman ('sibao', 'hassandaran'), who, however, is never the magic priest, sits quietly inhaling the narcotic smoke of the incense. Soon he rises, and to the beat of the drums begins to dance. This dance consists of convulsive movements of the hands and feet ; it grows more and more lively, and ends in convulsive leaps, the dancer breaking down exhausted. He has now become a new man, and sees the spirit in question coming to him in its earlier human form. He is no longer sensible of his own

---

[1] Cf. N, p. 45 A medical missionary in Pekin, interested in these matters, endorsed this from his own experience in a conversation I had with him He had been unable to make the investigations he desired owing to this very fact. He said that the reticence of the Chinese themselves on the subject makes it very difficult to obtain detailed information about it. They are thoroughly ashamed of its existence amongst them.

[2] N, p 58   [3] W, p. 75   [4] W, p. 71 ff

[5] Cf. the account of Elisha calling for a minstrel in order to 'work up' the prophetic frenzy, 2 Kings iii. 15. 16 a. Cf also 1 Sam x. 5

body; his feeling and thought are those of the dead. The men around him seem to him small, red in colour; he feels giddy. In his exhaustion palm wine and betel are given to him. Frenziedly he swallows often handfuls of the sharpest pepper. Before asking counsel of the spirit that appears in him the medium is tested as to whether the spirit who is summoned is really speaking through him or whether he is feigning it. The relatives inquire about family secrets, about far away members of the family, and about circumstances known only to the nearest survivors. Should the possessed person approve himself by fitting answers the reason why he has been called is stated, and he is asked why he is angry, and what must be done to avert the calamity. The demands of the dead, whatever they are, must be met. Spirits are summoned in order to reveal where things lost or strayed men may be found. . . . The medium is frequently also the foreteller of coming events. Thus from the statements of some old Battak Christians, some years before the appearance of the first missionary, a medium foretold his coming and exhorted his grandchildren to hearken to the good message of the foreign men.' 'The ecstatic condition is often, though not always, furthered by artificial means such as incense, drum-beating, and dancing. A medium, however, is frequently possessed without these. The medium is much exhausted by his efforts. Not infrequently at the beginning of his career he falls ill and dies; such people it is said never reach old age.[1] . . . No one becomes a medium through study (like the datu). The spirit himself chooses his own media. . . . The medium receives nothing [i.e. no payment]. When he dies a successor is not appointed by election or any human mediation, but only by the entrance of the spirit.' According to Warneck Shamanism is found amongst many peoples.[2] He proceeds, 'Battak Christians who were themselves in former days media, have sometimes, against their will, fallen

---

[1] Cf. C, p. 113 'The medium is never long-lived.' Cf. also Pierre Janet, *L'Automatisme psychologique*, 8me éd, p. 406.

[2] He gives a long list of them. For voluntary possession among the Dravidians of India, see E, p. 52. Note that it is not the 'bhutavaidyadu' (i.e. demon doctor) but the diviner who goes into the trance and becomes possessed. There seems to be a large element of fraud in the proceedings described by Elmore.

back into the possessed state. When, as they say, "they became men again", they were made profoundly miserable by their fall, and they assured me that they must have been acting under a constraint which they could not resist. . . . The descending spirit makes use of special language, the words of which, like that of the funeral songs, are partly para-phrases, partly obsolete, and not understood by every one. . . . Sometimes the medium may not have known the dead man whose consciousness has replaced his own. One who was born a Christian reported two cases in which women on whom the spirit had alighted read Battak writings fluently in their ecstatic condition, though in their normal state they could not read. People who at other times can scarcely read display great eloquence in the possessed state.' [1]

In the above we may observe three important factors which may be present in the condition of the possessed person or the person in trance:

(*a*) Another personality seems to be speaking through him.
(*b*) He is largely anaesthetic (cf. swallowing of pepper).
(*c*) He gives evidence of supernormal knowledge.

With the foregoing, mainly concerned with group (1), we may compare evidence from China which would fall in group (2), 'involuntary possession'.

In a communication to Nevius a Chinese scholar, Chen Sin Ling, writes as follows: [2] 'When a man is thus afflicted, the spirit (kwei) takes possession of his body without regard to his being strong or weak in health. It is not easy to resist the demon's power. Though without bodily ailments, pos-sessed persons appear as if ill. When under the spell of the demon they seem different from their ordinary selves. In most cases the spirit takes possession of the man's body con-trary to his will, and he is helpless in the matter. The kwei has the power of driving out the man's spirit, as in sleep or dreams. When the subject awakes to consciousness he has not the slightest knowledge of what has transpired. The actions of possessed persons vary exceedingly. They leap about and toss their arms, and then the demon tells them

---

[1] It will be seen that the latter part of this description refers to a state not necessarily voluntarily induced.

[2] N, p. 45 ff.

E

what particular spirit he is, deceitfully calling himself a god,
or one of the genii come down to the abodes of mortals.   Or
it professes to be the spirit of a deceased husband or wife, or
a hu-sien ye (one of the fox fraternity).   There are also kwei
of the quiet sort who talk and laugh like other people, only
that the voice is changed.   Some have a voice like a bird.
Some speak Mandarin [Mandarin is the spoken language of
the northern provinces of China, and is quite different from
the language of the province of Fukien from which this communication comes], and some the local dialect; but though
the speech proceeds from the mouth of the man, what is said
does not appear to come from him.   The outward appearance
and manner are also changed. . . . As to the outward appearance of persons possessed, of course, they are the same
persons as to outward form, as at ordinary times; but the
colour of the countenance may change, the demon may cause
the subject to assume a threatening air, and a fierce, violent
manner.   The muscles stand out on the face, the eyes are
closed, or they protrude with a frightful stare.   Sometimes
the possessed person pierces his face with an awl, or cuts his
tongue with a knife.   In all these mad performances the
object of the demon is to frighten people. . . . When they
take possession of a man, if they personate a scholar, they
affect a mild and graceful literary air; if they personate men
of warlike reputation, they assume an air of resolution and
authority.   They first announce their name, and then act so
that men will recognize them, as being what they profess to
be.   The words spoken certainly proceed from the mouths of
the persons possessed; but what is said does not appear to
come from their minds or wills, but rather from some other
personality, often accompanied by a change of voice; of this
there can be no doubt.   When the subject returns to consciousness he invariably declares himself ignorant of what he
has said.'

The following is part of the description of possession by
Wang Wu-Fang,[1] another of Nevius' correspondents: 'Cases
of demon-possession are found among persons of robust
health, as well as those who are weak and sickly. . . . In

---

[1] A 'greatly respected native helper connected with the English Baptist
Mission of Shan-tung.' See N, p. 52 f.

many cases of possession the first symptoms occur during sleep, in dreams. The subject is given to weeping. When asked a question he answers in a word or two, and then falls to weeping again. He perhaps asks that incense, or paper money, may be burned, or for other sacrificial offerings ; or he complains of heat or cold. When you give the demon what it wants the patient recovers. In a majority of cases of possession the beginning of the malady is a fit of grief or anger [1] The outward manifestations are apt to be fierce and violent. It may be that the subject alternately talks and laughs ; he walks awhile and then sits ; or he rolls on the ground, or leaps about ; or exhibits contortions of the body, and twistings of the neck. . . . When the demon has gone out, and the subject recovers consciousness, he has no recollection whatever of what he has said or done. This is true invariably.'

It will be well to quote from one more of the communications to Nevius in response to his questionary. Wang Yung-ngen of Pekin writes :[2] 'It may be said in general of possessed persons, that sometimes people who cannot sing are able when possessed to do so ; others who ordinarily cannot write verses, when possessed compose in rhyme with ease. Northern men will speak languages of the south, and those of the east the language of the west ; and when they awake to consciousness they are utterly oblivious of what they have done.'

The following is an extract from the summary which Nevius makes of the whole of the evidence which he has collected :[3] ' During transition from the normal to the abnormal state, the subject is often thrown into paroxysms, more or less violent, during which he sometimes falls on the ground senseless, or foams at the mouth, presenting symptoms similar to those of epilepsy or hysteria. . . . During the transition period the subject often retains more or less of his normal consciousness. The violence of the paroxysms is increased if the subject struggles against, or endeavours to repress, the abnormal symptoms. When he yields himself up to them

[1] In China a violent fit of anger appears to be a very common prelude to the appearance of the phenomena of possession Cf., e. g , C, pp. 116 and 120.
[2] N, p. 58.   [3] N, p. 143 ff.

the violence of the paroxysms abates, or ceases altogether.
. . . The most striking characteristic of these cases is that
the subject evidences another personality, and the normal
personality for the time being is partially or wholly dormant
The new personality presents traits of character utterly different from those which really belong to the subject in his
normal state, and this change of character is with rare excep-
tions in the direction of moral obliquity and impurity. Many
persons while "demon-possessed" give evidence of knowledge
which cannot be accounted for in ordinary ways. They often
appear to know of the Lord Jesus Christ as a Divine Person,
and show an aversion to, and fear of, Him. They sometimes
converse in foreign languages of which in their normal states
they are entirely ignorant. . . . Many cases of "demon-possession" have been cured by prayer to Christ, or in His name,
some very readily, some with difficulty. So far as we have
been able to discover, this method of cure has not failed in
any case, however stubborn and long continued, in which it
has been tried. And in no instance, so far as appears, has
the malady returned, if the subject has become a Christian,
and continued to lead a Christian life.'[1]

From a perusal of the above evidence we see that the three
important factors (*a*), (*b*), and (*c*), noted in group (1), are
equally present in group (2). Thus in group (2) we may
recognize the characteristics (*a*), (*b*), and (*c*), and in addition
the following·

- (*d*) Demon possession not dependent on state of physical
  health.
- (*e*) An attack is followed by amnesia as to speech and
  action during it.
- (*f*) Behaviour during an attack usually violent, though
  occasionally lachrymose, mild, or cheerful.
- (*g*) The patient often exhibits a change of outward appearance to some extent corresponding to the nature of
  the possessing 'spirit'.

(*h*) He often shows supernormal ability [in addition to (*e*)
'supernormal knowledge'].

I do not wish to maintain that these additional characteristics noted in group (2), 'involuntary possession', are never

[1] Contrast Warneck on the Battaks of Sumatra (above, p. 64 f.).

present in cases which fall in group (1), 'voluntary possession'. On the contrary it is likely that some, if not all, are
often thus present. For example, it is *a priori* extremely
probable that the medium on return to his normal condition
after having been in a state of 'possession' deliberately
induced is entirely unconscious of what he has done or said
during that period; for this is characteristic of genuine
mediums in spiritualistic séances.

The above analysis brings us to a conclusion of considerable importance. The possessed person of group (1)
exhibits phenomena exhibited by the medium at a spiritualistic séance :[1] the chief characteristics of group (1) are all
found in group (2). It therefore appears likely that in dealing
with the problem of demon possession we are dealing with
one identical with that of the spiritualistic séance.[2]

Before leaving the evidence from the mission-field I will
give two accounts of possession recorded by Miss Cable.
They are interesting because they are good illustrations of
the phenomena tabulated above. The first shows in many
respects a curious similarity to that of the Gerasene Demoniac.
It runs thus:[3] 'Our first woman patient in Hwochow Opium
Refuge became interested in the Gospel, and on her return
home destroyed her idols, reserving, however, the beautifully
carved idol shrines which she placed in her son's room. Her
daughter-in-law who occupied this room . . . desired to become
a Christian and gave us a warm welcome whenever we could
go to the house. About six months later we were fetched by
special messenger from a village where we were staying to
see this girl who was said to be demon possessed. We found
crowds of men and women gathered to see and to hear. The
girl was chanting the weird minor chant of the possessed,
the voice, as in every case I have seen, clearly distinguishing
it from madness. This can perhaps best be described as
a voice distinct from the personality of the one under possession. It seems as though the demon used the organs of
speech of the victim for the conveyance of its own voice.

[1] See the next section.
[2] The evidence seems to point in this direction. I should, however, make
it clear that I do not pretend to have given a scientific proof that this conclusion
is correct.
[3] C, p. 118 f.

She refused to wear clothes or to take food, and by her
violence terrorised the community. Immediately upon our
entering the room with the Chinese woman evangelist she
ceased her chanting, and slowly pointed the finger at us,
remaining in this posture for some time. As we knelt upon
the "kang" to pray, she trembled and said, "the room is
full of gwei;[1] as soon as one goes another comes." We en-
deavoured to calm her, and to make her join us in repeating
the sentence, " Lord Jesus, save me ". After considerable
effort she succeeded in pronouncing these words, and when
she had done so we commanded the demon to leave her,
whereupon her body trembled and she sneezed some fifty or
sixty times, then suddenly came to herself, asked for her
clothes and some food, and seemingly perfectly well resumed
her work. So persistently did she reiterate the statement
that the demons were using the idol shrines for a refuge,
that during the proceedings just mentioned her parents
willingly handed over to the Christians present these valuable
carvings, and joined with them in their destruction. From
this time onwards she was perfectly well, a normal, healthy
young woman.'

The second is as follows:[2] 'A spirit may take temporary
possession of a human body in order to find a means of
expression for some important communication, and after
delivering its message leave the person unconscious of that
which has taken place. An instance of this occurred in a
family with which I am intimate. The eldest daughter was
married into a home where she received ill treatment from
her mother-in-law. For several years she was systematically
underfed and overworked, and when at last she gave birth to
a son we all expected she would receive more consideration.
The hatred of her mother-in-law was, however, in no degree
abated, and when the child was a month old she brought her

---

[1] '"Gwei" [= *kwei* in the accounts from Nevius] is the term used by the
common people to indicate the being whose influence is feared by all, and who
receives from every family some measure of propitiatory sacrifice. We read in
the " Uh chao chuan " or " Divine Panorama " that "every living being, no
matter whether it be a man or an animal, a bird or a quadruped, a gnat or a
midge, a worm or an insect, having legs or not, few or many, all are called
gwei after death."' C, p. 110.
[2] C, p. 116 f.

daughter a meal of hot bread in which the girl detected an unusual flavour which made her suspicious. She threw the remainder to the dog, and before many hours had passed both the unfortunate girl and the dog were dead. Her father was away from home at the time, the young men of the family meanwhile carrying on the work of the farm. A few days later her brothers and first cousins, strong, vigorous young farmers, being together in the fields, her cousin, aged 22, suddenly exhibited symptoms of distress. He trembled and wept violently. Those with him becoming alarmed at so unusual a sight went to his assistance, intending to take him home. He wept, however, the more violently, saying, " I am Lotus-bud ; I was cruelly done to death. Why is there no redress ? " Others of the family were by this time at hand, and recognising the effort made by the girl's spirit to communicate with her own people whom she had had no opportunity of seeing in the hour of her death, spoke directly to her as though present. Telling her the facts of the case, they explained that all demands must remain in abeyance until her father's return, when the guilty party would be dealt with by her family whose feeling was in no sense one of indifference. In about an hour's time the attack passed, leaving the young man exhausted and unconscious of what had taken place. Miss Cable goes on to narrate how the requirements of redress were fulfilled.

C. *Demon Possession viewed in the Light of Morbid Psychology and of Psychotherapy.*

In the foregoing section I have spoken of 'genuine mediums'. By this I mean ' mediums ' who exhibit unusual and striking phenomena without the aid of conscious trickery. In view of the disrepute into which mediumship has fallen in the eyes of many thinking men owing to the constant discovery of fraud it may be held that no such people exist.[1]

---

[1] This opinion will be strengthened by the recent fascinating book entitled *The Road to En-dor*, which shows how the seemingly most inexplicable phenomena may be faked. (See *The Road to En-dor, being an account of how two Prisoners of War at Yozgad in Turkey won their way to Freedom*, by E. H. Jones, I. A. R O [John Lane]).

I do not, however, think that this view can be maintained after a careful inquiry into the facts. Even if we were to confine our attention to professional mediums, in my opinion we should not be able to attribute in all cases their remarkable accomplishments to fraud;[1] but it is the evidence provided by the morbid cases of 'dissociation of personality' (investigated critically and scientifically by distinguished medical psychologists) in which 'mediumistic' powers are frequently manifested that forces us to admit the actual occurrence of phenomena which ordinary folk are accustomed to associate with spiritualistic séances.

I wish to show that there is a connexion between the condition of the 'demon possessed' and that of mediums in trance chiefly on account of the apparently supernormal knowledge which is often to be observed in both. The most plausible theory concerning this knowledge in mediums is that the medium gains it through 'tapping' the unconscious of the 'sitter'.[2] This was exemplified very prettily in a paper read by Miss Lily Dougall at the Church Congress meetings at Southend on 20 Oct. 1920. In it she recounts how that she visited a medium who gave her vivid descriptions of personages in the spirit world with whom she (the medium) was in communication. The accounts corresponded accurately and in detail, one with an acquaintance of Miss Dougall's who was still in the land of the living, and the other with a character in one of Miss Dougall's novels.[3] The

---

[1] Cf. the following concerning the celebrated medium Mrs Piper written by so critical an investigator as Frank Podmore: 'Partly, then, from the stringent nature of the precautions taken and the high measure of success nevertheless achieved, partly from the nature of the revelations themselves, we are led to the conclusion that Mrs. Piper's trance utterances indicate the possession of some supernormal power of apprehension—at lowest the capacity to read the unspoken, and even unconscious, thoughts and emotions of other minds' (*Modern Spiritualism*, vol. ii, p 342). See also the account of a series of 'sittings' with a medium in New York, by T. J. Hudson (*The Law of Psychic Phenomena*, p. 224 ff [1892]).

[2] It is possible that there may be some instances in which this theory does not cover the facts, and where, in lieu of the spiritistic hypothesis, we should have to suppose a 'tapping' of the unconscious of some one not present.

[3] See *The Times* of 21 Oct., 1920. I am given to understand that Miss Dougall had lunched with the 'acquaintance' in question just previously to going to the medium, and that on her way thither she had discussed with a friend the characters in the novel concerned. Cf. Émile Boirac, *The Psycho-*

case is interesting both as showing the medium's 'genuine-ness' (for a fraud would never have 'given herself away' so deliberately), and also as indicating the only source from which the descriptions could have been derived (i. e. Miss Dougall herself). Do we not find here a clue to the solution of what has often been held to be a difficulty in the Gospel story, viz., the 'knowledge' of Jesus which the demons are recorded to have possessed (cf. Mk. i. 34, iii. 11, &c.')? There are many signs in the Synoptics that during the earlier part of His ministry Jesus was exercised in mind as to His own Person and vocation. As far as we can judge, the cases of the healing of the possessed which are handed down to us belong to this period. If, as I believe and hope to show more clearly below, the state of 'possession' is a psychological state in which the subject displays a heightened 'sensibility' similar to that manifested by a person in trance, the recog-nition of our Lord by the demoniacs becomes easily intelligible. An examination of some of the pathological cases showing 'possession' symptoms which have been investigated within recent years will show, I believe, the probable nature of demon possession in N. T. times and at the present day in heathen lands, and will prove the above-mentioned hypothesis to be not altogether unwarrantable.

The thesis that I desire to maintain is put succinctly by Pierre Janet in two passages: 'La croyance à la possession n'est que la traduction populaire d'une vérité psychologique ',[2] and 'Le point essentiel du spiritisme c'est bien, croyons-nous, ainsi que le dit Gros Jean,[3] la désagrégation des phénomènes

logy of the Future, E. T., p 206 [E. T, 1918]: 'In spiritistic séances it is not unusual to establish the fact that the responses given by the table, the planchette, or the pencil, reflect not the thoughts of the medium but those of some one of the assistants, who is wholly surprised to see thus revealed publicly what he believed to be hidden deep within his own heart.'

[1] It is interesting to note that Dr. Menzies Alexander, maintaining that ' the confession of Jesus as the Messiah or Son of God is the classical criterion of genuine demonic possession ', concludes the lengthy and learned argument of his book by stating that the application of this criterion ' proves that genuine demonic possession was a unique phenomenon in the history of the world ; being confined indeed to the earlier portion of the ministry of our Lord ' (*Demonic Possession in the N. T.*, pp. 147 and 247).

[2] *L'Automatisme psychologique*, huitieme édition, p. 441.

[3] The reference is to an anonymous writing entitled ' Seconde lettre de Gros

psychologiques et la formation, en dehors de la perception personnelle, d'une seconde série de pensées non rattachée à la première.'[1]

A glance at the literature during the last hundred years dealing directly or indirectly with morbid psychology shows a quite surprising number of instances where people living during this period have been conscious of being 'possessed' by one or more different personalities—these personalities being sometimes beneficent, sometimes evil, the person afflicted being in a few cases 'possessed' by both varieties.[2]

The following case of Janet's is a very instructive example[3] (I quote from Frank Podmore's précis of it in *Modern Spiritualism*, vol. ii, p. 309 f.):

'Achille is a French peasant of bad family history, his mother, in particular, and her family having been given to drunkenness. Achille himself in his youth was feeble, delicate, and timid, but not markedly abnormal. He married at twenty-two, and all went well until one day in his thirty-third year, after returning home from a short absence, he became afflicted with extreme taciturnity, and in the end completely dumb. He was examined by various physicians, who successively diagnosed his ailment, one as diabetes, another as angina pectoris. Achille's voice now returned, he manifested symptoms appropriate in turn to either malady, and incessantly bewailed his sufferings. In the final stage, he fell into a complete lethargy, and remained motionless for two days. At the end of that period he awoke and burst into a fit of Satanic laughter, which presently changed into frightful shrieks and complaints that he was tortured by demons. This state lasted for many weeks. He would pour forth blasphemies and obscenities ; and immediately afterwards lament and shudder at the terrible words which the demon had uttered through his mouth. He drank laudanum and other poisons, but did not die ; he even tied his feet together, and threw himself into the water, ultimately coming safe to land. In

Jean à son évêque au sujet des tables parlantes, des possessions et autres diableries '. Paris, Ledoyen, 1855.

[1] Op. cit., p. 401.

[2] See, for example, besides the more celebrated cases, the instances quoted by Janet, op. cit., p. 441 f.

[3] *Névroses et Idées fixes*, vol. i, p. 377 et seq

each case he ascribed his deliverance to the fact that his
body was doomed to be for ever the abode of the damned.
He would describe the evil spirits which tormented him,
their diabolic grimaces, and the horns which adorned their
heads. Ultimately he came under Professor Janet's charge,
and the latter satisfied himself that the unhappy man had all
the signs of genuine possession as described by mediaeval
chroniclers; that his blasphemies were involuntary, and many
of his actions unconsciously performed. Janet even made the
devil write at his bidding—in French not too correctly spelt
—poor Achille the while knowing nothing of the matter; and
further established the fact that during the convulsive movements of the upper part of his body Achille's arms were
insensible to pricking and pinching—an old-time proof of
demoniacal possession. In the end this most guileful of
modern exorcists persuaded the devil, as a proof of his
power over the unhappy man, to send poor Achille to sleep;
and in that suggested sleep M. Janet interrogated the
demoniac, and learnt the secret of his malady. He had been
acting out for all these months the course of a most unhappy
dream. During the short absence which preceded his attack
he had been unfaithful to his wife. Possessed with a morbid
terror of betraying his fault, he had become dumb. The
physicians who had been called in had unwittingly suggested,
by their questions, the symptoms of one or two fatal maladies,
and his morbid dream-self had promptly seized upon the
hints, and realized them with surprising fidelity. In the slow
development of his uneasy dream the time came for the man
to die; and after death there remained for such a sinner as
he nothing but damnation. The lesser devils stuck nails into
the flesh, and Satan himself, squeezing through the holes so
made, entered on an ambiguous co-tenancy of the tortured
body. It is pleasant to record that the skilful exorcist was
able to dispel the evil dream, and restore the sufferer to his
right mind.'
   It is unnecessary to dwell upon the similarity between the
stranger symptoms in this case and the symptoms recorded
of the possessed in the N. T. and in heathen lands at the
present day. In passing it should be remarked that the story
of Achille shows very clearly that the theory maintained in
this essay that the paralysis of the 'sick of the palsy' was

really brought about by a sense of sin is not an absurd one.[1]

Again, we may note some of the symptoms manifested by the girl 'S. W.'—a case which was investigated by Dr. C. G. Jung in 1899 and 1900.[2] The patient was fifteen and a half years old. She had a bad heredity, many of her relations and forebears having been 'peculiar' in one way or another. Up till the age mentioned she had been fond of day dreaming, and apt to make curious verbal mistakes when reading, but, apart from this, she displayed 'no serious hysterical manifestations'.[3] In July 1899 she took part in some joking table-turnings with friends, and was discovered to be a good 'medium'. For weeks after this she frequently went into trance and exhibited most of the phenomena associated with mediums. The process, detailed at length by Jung, reached the maximum in four to eight weeks. 'Thenceforth', in Jung's words, 'a gradual decline was noticeable; the ecstasies grew meaningless and the influence of Gerbenstein[4] became more powerful. The phenomena gradually lost their distinctive features, the characters which were at first well demarcated became by degrees inextricably mixed. The psychological contribution grew smaller and smaller until finally the whole story assumed a marked effect of fabrication. Ivenes[5] herself was much concerned about this decline; she became painfully uncertain, spoke cautiously, feeling her way, and allowed her character to appear undisguised. The somnambulic attacks decreased in frequency and intensity. All degrees from somnambulism to conscious lying were observable. Thus the curtain fell'.[6]

The symptoms that concern us here and which I shall indicate briefly below belong to the period prior to the employment of conscious fraud. It would take too long to give Jung's explanation of them, and therefore it must suffice to say that he accounts for them (in my view successfully) on psychological and physical grounds, corroborating Janet's theses recorded above.

[1] See below, p. 88 ff.
[2] See Jung's *Collected Papers on Analytical Psychology*, E. T., 2nd ed, p. 16 ff
[3] p. 17.   [4] One of the 'spirits'.
[5] The name which 'S. W.' assumed for herself in trance.   [6] p. 83.

The symptoms to note are :

(1) A sense that she was possessed by various spirits (some-times when in this condition she speaks of herself in the third person) [pp. 18, 19, 25, 30, 31, &c.]

(2) She adopts the tone and gestures of the possessing 'spirit' in a remarkably lifelike way. Her movements depicted excellently her varying emotions [pp. 18 f., 28 ff.]

(3) She often fell into the 'possessed' state much against her will [p. 21].

(4) When 'possessed' she showed powers of speech not observed in her in the normal state. Thus, on one occasion, she 'made use exclusively of a literary German which she spoke with an ease and assurance quite contrary to her usual uncertain and embarrassed manner in the waking state'[p. 18]. At another time she spoke fluently in High German with a North-German accent[1] [p. 29] while again at another time she spoke the Swiss dialect [p. 32]. The language appears to have been consistently in agreement with what would have been expected of the 'spirit' in control at the moment.

(5) There was sometimes amnesia after the trance-conversation [p 27 ; cf p. 19 and pp. 33 and 34].

Many cases similar to the two outlined above might be cited. Flournoy's famous case of 'Hélène Smith',[2] one in many respects curiously parallel to that of 'S. W.', may be mentioned. The serious morbid condition of this patient seems to have started after she had joined a spiritualist circle, and was found to possess the attributes of a medium in an extraordinary degree. She, like 'S. W.', showed in trance a change in outward appearance approximating to the nature of the possessing 'spirit' ; in her case, too, there was amnesia after an attack. One of her most remarkable accomplishments was the speaking and writing freely (when in trance) of the 'Martian' language,[3] which was one which Podmore describes

---

[1] A frequent guest in 'S. W.'s' house was a gentleman who spoke High German [p. 32].

[2] See *Des Indes à la planète Mars* (1900). I rely for my information about this work upon Podmore's abstract in *Modern Spiritualism*, vol ii, pp. 315-22.

[3] 'In November, 1894, the spirit of the entranced medium was wafted—not without threatenings of sea-sickness—through the cosmic void, to arrive eventually on the planet Mars,' p, 316.

as a language which a young child might construct by substituting for each word in the French dictionary an arbitrary collocation of letters, and for each letter a new and arbitrary symbol. The remarkable thing was not the language, but the fact that the 'spirits' who employed it did so with freedom and fluency, and were consistent in their usage both of the spoken and of the written words. The feat of memory that made this possible must have been prodigious. Hélène appears to have come of healthy stock, and her own physical health was robust.¹ Flournoy gives no decided opinion, but is disposed to take the view that she possessed real telepathic and clairvoyant powers.

Dr. Morton Prince's *Beauchamp* case² must be alluded to briefly. The patient here, is an astonishing example of 'multiple personality'. In this instance there were no dealings with table-turnings and spiritualist séances. It is difficult to describe adequately in a few words the complications of the case, the well-marked and complete difference in character and behaviour of the various 'personalities'; their varying degrees of physical health, the miserable health of one, the moderate health of another, and the excessively exuberant health of a third;³ the abrupt transitions from one 'personality' to another; the diabolical tricks which 'Sally' ('B III') played on 'B I'; the different memories that the characters possessed; the varying degrees of knowledge that each had of the other;⁴ the whole story constitutes a drama of absorbing interest culminating in the final obtaining by Dr. Prince of the 'Real Miss Beauchamp'. Not only did the 'personalities' alternate, but 'Sally' and 'B I', at any rate, gave clear evidence of co-existence.⁵ On one occasion Sally (in an unusually chastened mood) acted as sick nurse to B I

---

¹ Cf. above, p. 68 (*d*).

² Described at length by Dr. Prince in *The Dissociation of a Personality* (Longmans).

³ Vid. op. cit., 2nd ed., pp. 17 and 287.

⁴ Cf., e.g., p. 184: 'B I knew nothing of either of the other two personalities; B IV knew apparently something, but really nothing directly, beyond scrappy isolated memories, of B I and nothing of B III; B III knew all about the acts of the other two, but the thoughts of B I only.' Of course as time went on they learnt more and more *about* one another through observing the results of their acts.

⁵ See e.g., pp. 33 f, 116 256 f, 471, 475.

in delirium. If ever one body was inhabited by more than one ego this would seem obviously to have occurred in the case of the unfortunate Miss ' Beauchamp ', and yet Dr. Prince has shown that such was not the fact, ·but that all the extraordinary phenomena therein exhibited must be explained as due to a 'disintegration' or splitting off of parts of the mind from the main stream of the consciousness, such split off groups being none the less inevitably related to the fundamental ego-complex.[1]

It has been my endeavour to show the essential connexion between mediumistic phenomena and possession phenomena as they may be observed in the world at the present day, and by implication the obvious connexion between these and the demon possession of N.T. and subsequent times.[2] My contention will be strengthened by a quotation from Dr. Morton Prince : '—' Quite a number of cases -of disintegrated or multiple personality have been observed, sufficient to establish beyond all doubt the bona fide character of the phenomena, as well as the general principles underlying their development. The cases thus far studied and reported have represented varying degrees of complexity of organization of mental states and independence of the personalities. In the simpler forms the secondary personalities are manifested through highly synthesised "automatic" or hypnotic phenomena, and are recognized only as subconscious states through so-called automatic writing, and kindred manifestations, or else as states of hypnosis. The state called " Mamie " in the case of Mrs. R., reported by the writer,[4] and those of Léontine and Léonore in the case of Madame B., described by Dr. Pierre Janet, are examples of this simpler class. In more fully developed forms the second personalities are identical with the trance states of mediums, like that of Miss " Smith ", studied by M. Flournoy, and that of Mrs. " Smead ", studied by Professor Hyslop. In such cases the second personality does not obtain a completely independent existence, but comes out · of its shell, so to speak, only under special conditions when

[1] Cf. Jnng, *Analytical Psychology*, 2nd ed , p. 80.
[2] I have not felt it necessary to insist on the undoubted connexion of hypnotic phenomena or artificial somnambulic states with these things.
[3] Op. cit., p. 3 ff
[4] *Boston Med. and Surgical Journal*, 15 May 1890.

the subject goes into a "trance". The external life of personalities of this sort, so far as it is carried on independently of the principal consciousness, is extremely restricted, being confined to the experiences of the so-called "seance". Although such a personality is complete in having possession of the faculties of an ordinary human being, there is very little independence in the sense of a person who spontaneously and voluntarily moves about in a social world, and works, acts, and plays like any human being. It is questionable how far such a personality would be capable of carrying on all the functions of a social life, and of adapting itself to its environment. Hypnotic states, that is, artificially induced types of disintegration, are rarely, if ever, sufficiently complete, and possessed of adequate spontaneous adaptability to the environment to constitute veritable personalities.

'In the most fully developed forms, in cases like that of Felida X, reported by M. Azam ; of Louis Vivé, studied by several French observers ; and of Ansel Bourne, studied by Dr. Richard Hodgson and Professor William James, the disintegrated personality retains that large degree of complexity of mental organisation which permits complete, free, and spontaneous activity, approximating, at least, that of normal mental life. Though some cases exhibit glaring mental and physical defects, others may, to the ordinary observer, exhibit nothing more than an alteration of character and loss of memory for certain periods of life. Such persons often pass before the world as mentally healthy persons, though physically they may be neurasthenic. But a careful psychological examination will reveal deviations from the normal which show the true character of the alteration. It is to this last category that Miss Beauchamp belongs. In any one of her mental states she is capable of living her social life and doing her daily duties . . . . each personality leads its own life like any other mortal.' ·

VII

FEVER

Mk. i. 29–31; Lk. iv. 38–39; Mt. viii. 14–15.

Mk. ἡ δὲ πενθερὰ Σίμωνος κατέκειτο πυρέσσουσα
Lk. πενθερὰ δὲ τοῦ Σίμωνος ἦν συνεχομένη πυρετῷ μεγάλῳ
Mt. εἶδε τὴν πενθερὰν αὐτοῦ βεβλημένην καὶ πυρέσσουσαν

We shall be nearest the actual facts of this case if we follow Mk. Mt.'s setting of the incident is clearly artificial. As so often is the case with him, he abbreviates, and where he diverges from Mk. it is in the direction of a heightening of the miracle and an anachronistic reverence for our Lord.[1] Lk. also has the appearance of being less primitive than Mk. For example, there are verbal agreements which, in spite of considerable difference in detail, suggest dependence upon Mk.; also he omits the details about Andrew, James, and John, and introduces Simon into his narrative for the first time without comment. The force of his more definite terminology[2] in describing the case is weakened by his description of the method of cure, which, while it certainly indicates primitive thought, serves in effect to heighten the miracle, and implies a diagnosis of the disease which would hardly conduce to effective treatment.[3]

---

[1] Cf., e g. διηκόνει αὐτῷ for Mk.'s διηκόνει αὐτοῖς See J. M. Thompson, *M. N. T.*, p. 67. I think, however, that Mr. Thompson attributes much to the heightening of the miracle which is just as naturally and easily explained as due to abbreviation. Cf. Abbott's ingenious explanation of Mk.'s ἥψατο as due to the ambiguity of the Aramaic which employs the same word for 'touch' and 'draw near to' [= Heb. ‏נגע‎] (*The Fourfold Gospel*, Sect. III, p. 194).

[2] For πυρετὸς μέγας cf. Galen. Different. Febr..i. 1 (vii. 275) καὶ σύνηθες ἤδη τοῖς ἰατροῖς ὀνομάζειν ἐν τούτῳ τῷ γένει τῆς διαφορᾶς τὸν μέγαν τε καὶ μικρὸν πυρετόν. (Hobart, op. cit., p. 3 f)

[3] Cf. Loisy, *E. S.* i, 455: 'Luc dramatise la scène et introduit une sorte d'exorcisme . . . le Sauveur menace la fièvre, comme il a menacé le possédé dans la synagogue, la fièvre s'en va. Si l'évangéliste a défini plus haut la maladie en style de médecin (πυρετῷ μεγάλῳ), ce dernier trait fait moins d'honneur à ses connaissances positives, puisqu'il prend la fièvre pour une sorte de démon.'

As has been said, when the preceding scene in the synagogue was under discussion, the events described in Mk. i. 21–34 form a sequence which does not appear to be artificial, and there is good reason for supposing that the relative setting of these incidents in Mk. (followed by Lk.) is historically correct. Here Mk. gives us a picture which does not, indeed, supply us with all the information we could desire, but which is nevertheless vivid and, so far as it goes, convincing. The little group comes from the service in the synagogue (where Jesus had just performed a remarkable cure) to the house of Simon, whose mother-in-law is lying on her bed stricken with a fever.[1] Simon and the others at once consult Jesus about her, and He goes to her, and grasping her by the hand raises her. Thereupon the fever leaves her, and she begins to wait upon them.

We may tabulate as follows:

> *Disease*: Fever.
> *Treatment*: Jesus grasps her by the hand and raises her.
> *Result*: Immediate cure and strength to continue her household duties.

But the account of the treatment in the text obviously does not give us all the details, and there are certain factors which we can conjecture without trespassing outside the realm of practical certainty. For instance, it is absurd to suppose that the whole cure was carried out in dumb show. We may be certain that Jesus spoke to the woman, and, without having any knowledge of what He said, we may be equally sure that His words were 'therapeutic'. The factor of His personality displayed through His look and His bearing must also be taken into account. In addition, we shall not be unreasonable if we conjecture that the patient had already been informed of the remarkable cure which Jesus had just returned from performing in the synagogue

---

[1] We must rest content with this meagre definition of her malady. We are not even told approximately how long she had been down with this sickness, althongh Mk.'s narrative almost hints that it had come on while the others were in the synagogue.

The father of Publius, governor of Malta, cured of fever and dysentery. Acts xxviii. 7, 8.

ἐγένετο δὲ τὸν πατέρα τοῦ Ποπλίου πυρετοῖς καὶ δυσεντερίῳ συνεχό-μενον κατακεῖσθαι

The incident occurs in a 'we-passage'. There is good reason for thinking probable that the writer was an eye-witness of the event. Note the plural πυρετοῖς (contrast Lk. iv. 38). It is very likely employed to indicate an intermittent fever. But here, as in all the diseases mentioned in the N.T., our diagnosis must be to some extent conjectural. The older medical writers, such as Hippocrates, seem to have used the plural also in a more general sense of 'fever', the usage having probably originated from the observation of recurring and intermittent forms of the complaint.[1] However, the coupling of the word with dysentery suggests that the above-mentioned intermittent fever is meant.[2] Paul effects the cure by prayer and the laying of his hands on the man.

When we are considering the psychological effect of the reputation of a healer as predisposing to a cure we notice an interesting parallel between the conditions under which the present healing was brought about and those which are recorded in the case of Peter's mother-in-law. The bearing upon one another of the incidents described in Mk. i. 21-34 and prls. (the cure of the demoniac in the synagogue at Capernaum, of Peter's mother-in-law's fever, and subsequently of the various diseases of the crowd) has already been remarked. The present section, Acts xxviii. 1-10, provides us with a similar psychological situation. Verses 3-6 describe how Paul gained an immense reputation through suffering no ill consequences from a snake-bite; this event is followed by Paul's curing Publius's father of fever and dysentery (verses 7 and 8); and this in turn leads to the sick of the island in general coming and being healed[3] (ver. 9).

---

[1] See *E. B.* 1105, also Souter, *Pock. Lex.*, sub πυρετός.
[2] But it should be noted that Hippocrates sometimes uses δυσεντερίη in con-junction with πυρετός. (See Hobart, op cit., p. 52 f.)
[3] It should, however, be noticed that it is not clear that Paul was the only member of the party who healed the many sick folk. Sir William Ramsay, indeed, thinks that it was Luke who did this. He lays stress on the distinction

'Fever' is a symptom rather than a disease. If the diseases from which the patients were suffering were cured by mental and spiritual treatment the symptom of fever would, no doubt, vanish too. It is, however, vain to attempt to adduce parallels where there is such an immense range of possible maladies from which these people may have been suffering.

There is a complaint known as 'hysterical fever', which Dr. Paul Dubois says is a phenomenon more frequent than is generally believed; but, to judge from Dr. Dubois' account of it, there seems to be very little likelihood that the patients described in the N. T. were afflicted with this.[1]

In the case in Acts 'fever' (or, 'fevers') is coupled with 'dysentery'. Fever is a common accompanying symptom of what is nowadays called dysentery. It is therefore quite possible that the patient was suffering from this latter disease. I have not found a clear parallel to quote if this is so. But it should be remembered that diarrhoea and other bowel disturbances are frequently conditioned by mental states.[2] Moreover fever is the outcome of disturbances of the arterial system, and we know that regulation of the blood-supply may be accomplished by suggestion.[3]

---

between the ἰάσατο of ver. 8 and the ἐθεραπεύοντο of ver. 9, maintaining that the latter is here used in its strict sense of 'received medical treatment', which would have reference to the activities of Luke rather than Paul. (See *Luke the Physician*, p. 16 f.)

[1] See *The Psychic Treatment of Nervous Disorders*, pp. 181-3.

[2] It is not necessary to give references to the innumerable examples of the power of suggestion, for instance, to put an end to constipation or to check diarrhoea. Few soldiers or sailors who have been in action will be ignorant of the fact that mental conditions affect these states.

[3] E.g., cf. above, p. 22, and below, pp. 122-3. Dr. Hadfield has succeeded in altering the temperature, as measured by the thermometer, of the hand of a patient 26° (from 68° F. to 94° F.). This he did in the course of 20 minutes, and by suggestion in the *waking* condition. (See ' The Influence of Suggestion on Body Temperature ', *The Lancet*, 10 July 1920.)

VIII

PARALYSIS

Mk. ii. 1–12; Lk. v. 17–26; Mt. ix. 1–8.

> Mk. καὶ ἔρχονται φέροντες πρὸς αὐτὸν παραλυτικὸν αἰρόμενον ὑπὸ τεσσάρων
>
> Lk. καὶ ἰδοὺ ἄνδρες φέροντες ἐπὶ κλίνης ἄνθρωπον ὃς ἦν παραλελυμένος
>
> Mt. καὶ ἰδοὺ προσέφερον αὐτῷ παραλυτικὸν ἐπὶ κλίνης βεβλημένον

There is much that is perplexing about this story, and in consequence it is the subject of many differing opinions amongst critics. This seems to be, however, a case in which recent research in morbid psychology may give some help towards an adequate interpretation of the narrative.

Doubt is thrown on the correctness of the chronological setting of the story. It is urged that the 'conflict-section' (Mk. ii. 1–iii. 6) in which it occurs consists of incidents of too uniform a colour to be other than artificially constructed, and that the questions therein discussed (power to forgive sins, companying with 'outsiders', fasting, the sabbath) are such as must have been of great moment in the Apostolic Age.[1] Further, it is maintained that the occurrence of the messianic title 'Son of Man' shows that the event must be antedated, since our Lord would never have given away the 'messianic secret' by employing it publicly at any rate before Caesarea Philippi.[2] This last argument would be strong if the phrase ὁ υἱὸς τοῦ ἀνθρώπου were certainly used here in a messianic sense. But, on the contrary, there is no certainty that this is so. Indeed, there is a strong body of opinion among recent scholars which abandons this conclusion.[3] Some critics hold

---

[1] Cf. Moffatt, *I. L. N. T.*, p. 231, and Menzies, *The Earliest Gospel.* ad loc.

[2] Cf Moffatt, ibid.

[3] The question is too large and complicated to enter into in detail here. The view which commends itself to me is that the phrase has not a uniform signification in the N. T., and that, for example, where it occurs (in a genuine setting)

that verses 5b–10 of Mk. are redactional, and that they are due to the Christological controversies of the primitive Church with the Jews.[1] But we have little right to reject the possibility of such a collision taking place ͵between Jesus and the representatives of official Judaism. Dr. Bacon (one of the above-mentioned critics) supports his contention by arguing that, if the event as narrated had actually occurred, this particular charge of blasphemy must have been brought up at the trial. To which it has been replied that the authorities could not bring this charge because the cure of the man could not be denied, and therefore (opinions being what they were as to the relation between sin and disease) the forgiveness could not be disproved.[2]

There do not appear to be sufficient grounds for doubting the accuracy of Mk. in placing the scene in Capernaum. If he is right here then also he can hardly be very far out in his chronological setting, for it is improbable that such an event could have taken place in Capernaum much later in the ministry. Mk. must certainly be correct in placing it before the cure of the man with the withered hand in the synagogue there.[3] Thus, if we do not take ὁ υἱὸς τοῦ ἀνθρώπου here as a messianic title, there is good reason for supposing that the incident is placed by Mk. in its correct position at least relatively to the rest of our Lord's ministry.

The Synoptists are at one in their general outline of the story, and in that part of it which is most important for our purpose they agree to a large extent verbally. There are a few small points where Mt. and Lk. agree as against Mk., which taken individually are insignificant, but taken together

in passages dealing with events prior to Caesarea Philippi, it does not bear a messianic connotation, but stands either for 'man' or for the personal pronoun 'I'. Cf. Jackson and Lake, *B. Chr.*, Pt. I, vol. i, p. 375, who think that in the passage in question it signifies 'man'. Dalman, op. cit.,p. 263 f., favours here a messianic meaning, but admits the possibility that it represents an original personal pronoun.

[1] Cf. B. W. Bacon, *Beginnings of Gospel Story*, p. 24 f.; Loisy, *E. S.*, i, pp. 87 f., 107 f., 479 f.

[2] For this argument, and also on the whole 'Son of Man' question, I am indebted to an as yet unpublished essay by my friend Mr. W. H. Cadman.

[3] Cf. Burkitt, *G. H. T.*, p. 68 ff., whose argument appears to me a strong one.

can scarcely be due to coincidence.[1]   The end of Lk. v. 17 is also worthy of attention. καὶ δύναμις κυρίου ἦν εἰς τὸ ἰᾶσθι.. αὐτόν. With this we may compare Mt. ix. 8 ἰδόντες δὲ οἱ ὄχλοι ἐφοβήθη- σαν καὶ ἐδόξασαν τὸν θεὸν τὸν δόντα ἐξουσίαν τοιαύτην τοῖς ἀνθρώποις.[2] It seems just possible that these two passages have the same source.   Whether or not this is so, they are both interesting, because neither has a parallel in Mk., and both apparently belong to a primitive tradition, since there is in them a con- spicuous absence of developed Christological theories.

These small points prove nothing definite, but they suggest that Mt. and Lk. employed here either a primitive source in addition to Mk., or at least an edition of Mk. differing in certain particulars from that which we possess.[3]

Doubt has been thrown on the story owing to the seemingly insuperable difficulties of Mk.'s account of the way in which the paralytic was placed at the feet of Jesus.   This seems to have been a puzzle from very early days, and is probably enough the reason for Mt.'s complete omission of this feature of the story and for the way in which Lk. avoids much of Mk.'s harshnesss without really making clear what happened when he describes it.   The greatest stumbling-block is Mk.'s ἐξορύξαντες.   The awkwardness of this word doubtless accounts for its absence in D.[4]   The most happy conjecture is that of Wellhausen. who suggests that ἀπεστέγασαν τὴν στέγην is a misunderstanding of an Aramaic phrase which means 'they brought him up on to the roof'.[5]   If this is so ἐξορύξαντες may be a clumsy attempt to make intelligible a falsely rendered

---

[1] I give the refs. in Mt : verses 2 (ἰδοὺ . . . ἐπὶ κλίνης . . . εἶπεν), 5 (περιπάτει), 7 (ἀπῆλθεν εἰς τὸν οἶκον αὐτοῦ), also Mt. ver. 8 and Lk. ver. 26, where 'fear' is mentioned (not noted by Mk.).

[2] The context implies that the ἐξουσία is that of being able to cause the man to walk rather than to forgive his sins, although possibly the two ideas were inseparable in the mind of the writer.

[3] B. Weiss, in his reconstruction of Q, suggests the possibility of Mt. ix. 1-8 = Lk. v. 17-26 belonging to that document, indeed, he seems definitely to attribute the Matthaean version to it.   In this he does not appear to have much following.   (See Moffatt, *I. L. N. T.*, p 202, whence I obtain these par- ticulars.)

[4] See Wright's *Synopsis of the Gospels in Greek*, in loc.

[5] Wellhausen, *Das Evang. Marci*, p. 16.   The Aramaic phrase he suggests is arimuhi leggâra.   It should be noted that Wellhausen considers the chief difficulty to lie not in the word ἐξορύξαντες but in ἀπεστέγασαν τὴν στέγην.

Aramaic original.[1] But, in any case, the difficulties of this
passage are not of such a nature as to justify the rejection of
the main part of the story as spurious.

In this account, as in so many other of the healing narratives
in the Gospels, the focus of interest is not the miracle of
healing itself, but the controversy which arises out of the
situation. The way in which the power of healing is taken
for granted is very significant, and should be a warning
against the too easy assumption that our Lord's cures were
limited to a very restricted field of diseases. One more
important objection is brought by critics against this story,
and that is that here, contrary to the general Synoptic tradition,
Jesus is described as working a miracle in order to prove
a point. But we may well contend that in this respect the
Evangelists are misleading. It is reasonable to suppose that
the patient's paralysis was actually the outcome of a consciousness of guilt on his part, and that, when Jesus, with His
commanding, penetrating, sympathetic personality, and in an
intense atmosphere of faith and hope,[2] said τέκνον, ἀφίενταί σου
αἱ ἁμαρτίαι,[3] he believed it, with the result that his mental
'complex' was resolved, and the disappearance of its physical
manifestation (paralysis) would gradually and automatically
take place. In this case the gradual cure of the physical
symptoms was accelerated by further therapeutic action on
the part of the healer, viz., the definite order to get up and
walk. On this theory the cure was in all essentials performed
once the man believed that his sins were forgiven. If we
accept it, we may suppose that Jesus, whether by looking into
the man's face[4] or by some other means of gaining insight,

[1] Cf. II. G. Wood, *P. C.*, ad loc.
[2] Clearly the atmosphere was intense and expectant. Mk., however we
interpret the details of the scene, makes it obvious that the situation was of a
thoroughly dramatic character, and such as to arouse the expectancy and
'suggestibility' of the patient. Note that in the narrative Jesus remarks the
faith not of the sick man but of the four who carry him. This faith is sufficiently manifested by their dogged persistence. See below, p. 91, n. 1.
[3] 'Son, thy sins are forgiven.' This is preferable to Lk.'s ἄνθρωπε, ἀφίωνται
κ.τ.λ., even if on psychological grounds alone.
[4] Cf. Prof. Bleuler, *Studies in Word Association*, ed by C. G. Jung, trans.
by Dr. M. D. Eder, p. 5, n. 1 : 'Each single action represents the whole man .
the endeavour to deduce the whole man from his handwriting, physiognomy,
shape of the hand, his style, even the way he wears his shoes, is not altogether
folly.' Cf. Dr. Paul Hartenberg, *Physionomie et Caractère*.

saw what was the real cause of his suffering and so dealt with the malady at its roots.[1]

The brief exposition which has already been given [2] of the mechanism of 'hysteria' should, I think, show that this explanation of the event is not so far-fetched as it may sound. But first it should be observed that it removes certain difficulties in the story which are never satisfactorily dealt with in the commonly accepted theories. For instance, it explains what otherwise appears something almost like the unsympathetic irrelevancy of our Lord's affirmation of forgiveness when He saw the men's faith, while the one thing for which they were striving was the physical cure of the sufferer.[3] Further, it considerably modifies the extent to which this is an exception to the rule that our Lord never worked a miracle to prove a point or as a 'sign'. As has already been shown [4] there is good evidence that He wished to avoid a reputation as a great physician, since this would hinder Him in what He held to be His main task. It is therefore likely that He would have been glad to escape performing a cure on this very public occasion.[5] Seemingly, as it turned out, a striking miracle might have been avoided, because He was able to do all that was necessary to promote the ultimate recovery of the paralytic by such 'apt words' as 'have power to swage the tumours of a troubled mind' without causing any dramatic scene in public. But the incredulous controversy which was set going by His words determined Jesus, being deeply stirred by their lack of insight,[6] to show these doubters outwardly what He had in fact accomplished unbeknown to them.[7]

---

[1] Cf. N. Micklem, *The Galilean*, p. 45 f.

[2] Above, pp. 15–19.

[3] I do not feel that the conventional reply that He intended thus to teach the greater importance of spiritual well-being is quite satisfactory in the circumstances.

[4] See above, p. 45 f

[5] Note, the crowd was gathered in this house to listen to His teaching (Mk. ver. 2; Lk. ver 17).

[6] ? Another instance of ἐμβρίμησις.

[7] It does not concern our purpose to discuss whether Jesus claimed it His own peculiar right to forgive sins or it to be in the power of some or all of mankind generally to do so, or whether He was merely announcing the fact of Divine forgiveness. This last the disputers, at any rate, did not understand to be the case, for there would not be in that case any ground for a charge of

The interpretation that has been proposed for this case is that the patient's physical paralysis was the outcome of a mental or spiritual conflict with its accompanying sense of sin or guilt. If this is correct, no doubt the morbid physical symptoms were confirmed (and, likely enough, to a large extent induced) by the man's belief in the lasting wrath and condemnation of a stern and righteous God whose displeasure would always be upon him for his wickedness. Employing modern medical terminology we should then call this a case of hysterical paralysis, and an example of what we have called 'conversion hysteria'.[1]

In an earlier portion of this essay medical writers have been referred to as witnessing to the frequent psychic origin of paralysis. These witnesses can be multiplied. For example, Dr. Paul Dubois of Berne, who perhaps would not subscribe to the theory outlined above, may be quoted as one who asserts the fact—and that in no doubtful terms. 'Conditions of paralysis', he says, 'and of astasia-abasia form part of the symptomatology of hysteria. Everybody knows that these paralyses as localized in a functional muscular group, and appearing in the wake of a known or unknown autosuggestion, may disappear as if they were caused by suggestive influence. The fact is a commonplace one in the domain of hysteria.' He proceeds to affirm that these states of motor helplessness may even be induced under the influence of a simple dream or occur suddenly under the influence of anger or spite. Thus he has seen paralysis of the right arm occur in a little girl who dreamed she had defended her dog when attacked by a cow, and had struck blow after blow at the aggressor.[3] As

blasphemy. With regard to the two former alternatives cf., e.g., on the one hand Dr. A. C. Headlam, *The Miracles of the N. T.*, p. 199, with Drs. Jackson and Lake, op. cit., p. 379, on the other. It is important to bear in mind that a claim to forgive sins would, in the thought of the time, be a claim to the exercise of a Divine prerogative, and not of a function of the Messiah (Cf Dalman, *The Words of Jesus*, p. 261 f., contra Joh. Weiss.)

[1] Dr. R. J. Ryle, arguing against the 'neurotic theory of the miracles of healing' in the *Hibbert Journal* for April 1907, says (p. 580) : ' We have to remember that this so-called hysterical paralysis is almost always met with in women and girls.' This statement may have seemed reasonable in 1907 . it is certainly not so in 1922

[2] *The Psychic Treatment of Nervous Disorders*, E. T., 6th ed , p. 375

[3] Ibid. In this connexion he refers to Grasset's case where the dream brought about the cure.

an example of anger as a cause he gives the case of a lady
who, after an altercation with her cook, was seized with
paraplegia. 'I found the patient in bed, very much disturbed
by what had happened. Her legs were in tetany when
stretched out, and the patient was incapable of making the
slightest movement. Sensibility to a prick ceased over the
whole cutaneous surface of the lower extremities, and the
anesthesia ceased suddenly at the fold of the groin. While
I made the examination the patient asked me : "Is it serious?"
...... "Serious! Not in the least; it is only a nervous
weakness brought on by emotion. In three days you will be
on your feet!" Then, taking her relatives to one side, I took
care to say to them : "You have heard that I have said she
will be cured in three days; I could have said three weeks,
three months, or more, for I have seen these paraplegias last
for years. It all depends upon the idea that the patient gets
into her head. Take care, then, to take it for granted that the
patient will be cured within the fixed time. Do not make
believe to believe it; that will not do; believe it—all of you
believe it!"[1] Without any further treatment the patient was
cured, and walked on the third day.'[2]

As a final example I will cite a case that came under the
notice of Dr. Hadfield. In this instance 'fear and the impulse
to run away conflicted in the/mind of the soldier with his sense
of duty, and ended in a condition of paralysis of the legs,
unconsciously produced, which solved the immediate problem
but brought about a breakdown in health.'[3]

Mk. iii. 1-6 ; Mt. xii. 9-14 ; Lk. vi. 6-11.

Mk. ἄνθρωπος ἐξηραμμένην ἔχων τὴν χεῖρα
Mt. ἄνθρωπος χεῖρα ἔχων ξηράν
Lk. ἡ χεὶρ αὐτοῦ ἡ δεξιὰ ἦν ξηρά

This story provides us with another example of a record
of healing wherein the stress is laid not upon the healing

---

[1] An interesting commentary upon the τὴν πίστιν αὐτῶν of Mk. ii. 5 prls.
[2] Op. cit., p. 376.
[3] *The Spirit*, ed. by Canon B. H. Streeter, p. 30 n. For further instances of
the working of the mechanism of hysteria as described above see Pfister, op. cit.,
pp. 31–44 and the table on pp. 56 and 57. See also M. D. Eder, *War-Shock*,
p. 71, who describes a case of paraplegia as a wish-fulfilment.

itself but upon the controversy which gathers around it—
in this instance about Sabbath observance. The incident
is the last in the so-called 'conflict-section' noted above,[1] of
which that of the 'sick of the palsy' was the first. But,
as there so here, there appears to be good ground for regarding
the Marcan (and Lucan) chronological setting as substantially
accurate in respect of the ministry as a whole.

Such a view does not preclude the opinion that the 'conflict-
section' is, to some extent, artificially arranged. What it does
maintain is that there is nothing intrinsically improbable about
the controversies described taking place at a comparatively
early stage in the ministry, and that Mk., while he does not
give us a detailed history of events, is not (at any rate here)
misleading us as to their general sequence. There is considerable force in Prof. Burkitt's argument that this incident
marks the final rupture of Jesus with the religious authorities
in Galilee,[2] and it is difficult not to agree with him when
he says that the general description of it must come from real
historical reminiscence. The narrative is 'totally unlike what
a Christian would have produced if he had been obliged to
rely on his imagination alone.'[3]

In the account of the healing we may again take Mk. as
supplying us with the most primitive evidence that we can
obtain. Mt., as usual, abbreviates, although he also introduces,
appropriately enough, a 'saying' (xii. 11–12) which is not here
present in any of its forms in the other two Synoptists. Lk.,
on the other hand, frequently expands the Marcan account,
but he also has some significant omissions. His expansions
are not such as to make probable an additional source. Thus,
we cannot set much store by ἑτέρῳ σαββάτῳ (ver. 6), while καὶ
διδάσκειν (ver. 6), οἱ γραμματεῖς καὶ οἱ Φαρισαῖοι (ver. 7), and αὐτὸς
δὲ ᾔδει τοὺς διαλογισμοὺς αὐτῶν (ver. 8) are all details with which
we are familiar elsewhere.[4] Hobart[5] says that δεξιά (ver. 6) is
a mark of particularity such as a physician would observe, and
that the medical writers invariably state whether it is the right
or left member that is affected. We may, however, see in this

---

[1] p 85.
[3] Ibid., p. 80 ff.
[2] See Burkitt, op cit, p 68 ff.
[4] Cf., e g., Mk. ii. 1-12. Note also, the Φαρισαῖοι of ver. 7 is inferred from Mk iii. 6.
[5] Op. cit., p. 7.

detail an indication of the physician and yet suspect him of a slight (and to him legitimate) indulgence of his imagination. In his account of the actual method of treatment there is nothing in his small additions which might not reasonably be inferred from the Marcan version. It is noteworthy that he omits (with Mt.) Mk.'s μετ' ὀργῆς συνλυπούμενος ἐπὶ τῇ πωρώσει τῆς καρδίας αὐτῶν,[1] and skilfully transfers the anger of Jesus to the onlookers. With Mt. he also omits mention of the Herodians.[2]

The emphasis of the story (as has been observed) is not on the wonder of the miracle, and hence we are deprived of information which is essential for a just estimate of the case. Did the patient ask to be cured ? Did he show faith on his side ? I have argued above that Jesus tried to avoid performing cures as far as was possible. If this contention was correct it is reasonable to suppose that in this instance the first move came from the sick man and not from our Lord. But it must be admitted that the narrative does not say so, and, in fact, implies the contrary. As it stands it does not, indeed, suggest that He worked the miracle to 'prove a point', but it does imply that He did it as a 'sign'. Jesus in the synagogue on the sabbath deliberately and provocatively fixes upon a man who is suffering from a physical complaint, calls him out, and proceeds publicly to cure him in order to demonstrate visually His teaching on the question of sabbath observance. Such is the impression which the Synoptists convey. I do not think that this is really compatible with the general picture that they give us of our Lord's methods. It is easy and, I think, legitimate to conjecture that the original features of the event have

---

[1] In estimating the significance of the word ὀργή we should remember Miss Dougall's warning that the report of our Lord's emotions 'has come to us through men soaked in the idea that moral wrath was half of human virtue and half of God ', and that the first-hand observers and reporters of His emotions ' had little power of analysis' and no ' precise nomenclature for emotions shading into one another'. She continues, ' When in a passion of grief at the insane blunders and self-destructive course of His opponents He told them truths that His profound insight revealed..of character ... how liable would His disciples be to call His emotion anger, themselves feeling angry on His behalf! and yet, in spite of all this, the predominating note of all we hear of His attitude towards sin is strong suffering and grief' (*The Practice of Christianity*, p. 92).
[2] See the pages from Burkitt cited above ; also Foakes Jackson and Lake, *B. Chr.*, Pt. I, vol. i, p. 119 f.

been distorted, owing to the fact that the Evangelists had focussed their attention almost exclusively on the controversy without giving due proportion to all the elements in the whole scene as a simple historical record. No doubt, in giving a broad view of the ministry, they were right in their emphasis.

We may tabulate the evidence that we have as follows:

Disease : ' Dried up ' or ' withered ' hand.

Treatment . The man is ordered to come out into the view of all present (ἔγειρε εἰς τὸ μέσον).

[Jesus asks the onlookers whether it is right on the Sabbath to do good or to do harm, to save life or to kill. They are silent.] Glancing round upon them with grieved indignation at their callousness, He says to the patient : Stretch out your hand.

Result : The man obeys, with the result that his hand is (immediately) restored.

The information supplied is not sufficient to allow of our making a diagnosis with any degree of confidence. The following is the account of the case which Dr. R. J. Ryle gives as being the most reasonable supposition from the data provided : [1]

' In the story of the man with the withered hand it is prob- able that we have to do with another case of paralysis; and, if so, we may assume with considerable confidence that the case was one of "infantile paralysis". This is the affection to which, at the present day, nearly all the instances of " withered hand " or of " withered leg " are owing. A child who has been in good health, or has suffered, perhaps, from a few days of feverishness, is found to have lost power in an arm or leg. The limb hangs flaccid and motionless. The muscles are found to be wasting when the limb is examined a week or two later, and the limb to be cold. For a month or two there may be a little recovery of movement. This soon stops, and the arm or leg remains ever after more or less powerless, and shrunken and cold. Normal growth is largely checked, and, in addition to the actual atrophy and arrest of development, various contractions and deformities become established as

[1] *The Hibbert Journal*, April 1907, p. 581 f.

time goes on. After death, the muscles are found to have
become much diminished and shrunken, and throughout a
certain portion of the spinal cord, corresponding with the
affected limb, destructive changes are found to have occurred
where the normal structure of ganglion cells and nerve-fibres
is replaced by the remains of the inflammatory process which
has been the cause of the palsy. Such is the ordinary history
of a withered hand. Here the very word "withered", which
aptly describes the condition of the limb, is the most appropriate description of the result of the process which has taken
place. If such was the pathology of the case described in
Mk. iii. 1, it is needless to say that, although it belongs to the
group of the nervous diseases, it does not belong to that class
of nervous disease which admits of treatment by moral impression or emotional shock.'

The affection which Dr. Ryle describes is what would be
called in more technical language 'Anterior Poliomyelitis',[1]
and is, as he shows, definitely an organic disease and not
merely functional. It will be noted that the disability indicated
is not confined to the hand alone, but of necessity affects the
arm as well.[2]

In our case the man is told to stretch out his hand, i. e.
inevitably, to stretch out his arm. If we are going to give any
meaning at all to 'withered' we must understand at least some
degree of wasting in the hand. Given a wasting of the hand,
whether we accept Dr. Ryle's diagnosis or whether we suppose
a functional paralysis, it is extremely improbable that the
affection was localized exclusively in that member.[3] It therefore follows almost certainly that the cure was, at least in part,
already performed when the patient obeyed the injunction to
stretch out his arm.

Although the diagnosis which Dr. Ryle suggests is, perhaps,
the most natural one in view of the description 'withered', it

---

[1] Cf. the account of ' Acute Poliomyelitis ' in Latham and Torrens, *Medical
Diagnosis*, p. 557 f

[2] Wetterstrand claims to have improved very considerably in 1890 the condition of a boy of 10 suffering from a disease which he diagnoses as ',poliomye-
litis acuta ' (a slight muscular atrophy of the whole right arm was to be
observed). See *Hypnotism and its Application to Practical Medicine*, by Otto
Georg Wetterstrand, M D , p. 27 f. (1897). Too much reliance must not, however, be put upon Wetterstrand's diagnosis.

[3] Perhaps this statement should be somewhat modified. See next page.

is certainly not the only possible one. The case might well be one of functional paralysis. Dr. A. F. Hurst, speaking of hysterical contractures and paralysis, says that they 'may result from injuries to the soft parts of the limb, with or without the bones and joints being involved. The commonest cause is a wound of the hand, foot, forearm, or leg, the symptoms generally developing below and above the injury as well as in its immediate neighbourhood. In many cases no nerve is involved, but in others temporary concussion of one or more peripheral nerves or of the brachial plexus may have occurred, or they may have received some actual injury of a recoverable nature. The severity of the symptoms does not vary with the degree of infection or the extent of the injury, which is often trivial. They are very rarely associated with severe wounds. . . . We have observed contractures and paralysis . . . in the absence of actual wounds—as, for example, in fractures, dislocations, sprains, and contusions.'[1] He proceeds to mention other factors in the aetiology of such contractures and paralyses, among which we may note his experience of three cases following on superficial burns, and seven cases in which the hysterical contracture appeared to be the sequel of localized tetanus.[2] 'In many cases', he continues, 'a single segment of a limb is involved, the hand and foot being most frequently concerned.[3] Very often, however, the whole or greater part of the limb is affected, but in such cases the contracture and paralysis are most severe in the immediate neighbourhood of the injury, although in rare instances the whole limb is completely paralysed and rigid.'[4] Dr. Hurst shows, with special reference to the hand, that in such cases there may be a diminution in the size of the member as the result of a deficient circulation. 'The normal circulation through a limb depends upon its active movements, the afferent nerve-fibres from the muscles probably giving rise to localized reflex vasodilatation. If for any reason the arm is not moved in cold weather, the hand becomes shrivelled, white or blue, numb, painful, and stiff. These well-recognized changes disappear at once with active exercise and on warming the limb,

---

[1] *S. H. N. S.*, vol. i, No. 5, pp. 248 50.   [2] Ibid.
[3] See above, p 95, and n. 3 on that page.
[4] Ibid., p. 250.

both of which restore the circulation. The tendency to disturbances of this kind is much greater in people with a poor
circulation than in those with a naturally good circulation. . . .
It is thus natural for the immobility caused by paralysis
or contracture of a limb, whether organic or hysterical, to
result in deficient circulation and the same secondary changes.
As, however, the paralysis is continuous, whereas the physio-
logical inactivity referred to only lasts for a few minutes or
at most for a few hours at a time, the secondary results are
likely to become much more profound, especially in individuals
with a poor circulation. The deficient circulation is generally
congenital, but in soldiers it is often acquired or aggravated as
result of exposure. Thus, in all cases in which circulatory
complications are severe, the circulation in the normal hand
is also feeble. The limb, especially its peripheral part,
becomes cold and white or blue, and the diminished blood-
supply results in a diminution in the volume of the hand,
except in the cases in which oedema develops.'[1] It seems to
me by no means unlikely that common folk in N.T. times,
seeing a man suffering from a trouble of the above kind, would
describe him (if they spoke Greek) as ἄνθρωπος ἐξηραμμένην
ἔχων τὴν χεῖρα.

In view of the foregoing discussion the following extract
from the *Journal* of one John Banks (1637-1710), under date
1677, is interesting [2]

'About this time, a Pain struck into my Shoulder, which
gradually fell down into my Arm and Hand, so that the Use
thereof I was wholly depriv'd of; and not only so, but my
Pain greatly encreas'd both Day and Night; and for three
Months I could neither put my Cloathes on nor off myself,
and my Arm and Hand began to wither, so that I did seek to
some Physicians for Cure, but no Cure could I get by any of
them ; until at last, as I was asleep upon my Bed, in the Night
time, I saw in a Vision, that I was with dear George Fox ;
and I thought I said unto him, George, my Faith is such, that
if thou seest it thy way to lay thy Hand upon my Shoulder,
my Arm and Hand shall be whole throughout. Which
remained with me after I Awaked, two Days and Nights (that

---

[1] Ibid., p. 252.
[2] Taken from the edition of George Fox's *Journal* published by the Cam-
bridge University Press and edited by Norman Penney, vol. ii, p. 466 f.

the thing was a true Vision) and that I must go to G. F.
until at last, through much Exercise of Mind, as a near and
great Tryal of my Faith, I was made willing to go to him; he
being then at Swarthmoore, in Lancashire, where there was
a Meeting of Friends, being on the first day of the Week.
And some time after the Meeting, I called him aside into the
Hall, and gave him a Relation of my Concern as aforesaid,
shewing my Arm and Hand; and in a little time, we walking
together Silent, he turned about, and looked upon me, lifting
up his Hand, and laid it upon my Shoulder, and said, The
Lord strengthen thee both within, and without. And so we
parted, and I went to Thomas Lowers of Marsh Grange that
Night; and when I was sate down to Supper in his House,
immediately, before I was aware, my Hand was lifted up to do
its Office, which it could not for so long as aforesaid; which
struck me into a great Admiration, and the next day I went
home, with my Hand and Arm restor'd to its former use and
strength, without any pain. And the next time that G. F. and
I met, he readily said, John, thou mended, thou mended;
I Answer'd, yea, very well, in a little time. Well, said he,
give God the Glory.'

Acts ix. 32-35.

εὗρεν δὲ ἐκεῖ ἄνθρωπόν τινα ὀνόματι Αἰνέαν ἐξ ἐτῶν ὀκτὼ κατα-
κείμενον ἐπὶ κραβάττου, ὃς ἦν παραλελυμένος.

With the two foregoing cases we may group this of the
cure of Aeneas at Lydda by Peter. There is a striking
similarity between the description of this case and that of the
Capernaum paralytic. All we can say is that in the light
of the experience of medicine and psycho-therapeutics cited in
respect of the two cases just dealt with there is nothing
intrinsically improbable about this one.

Peter's words to the patient appear to be psychologically
very apt.

Αἰνέα, ἰᾶταί σε Ἰησοῦς Χριστός· ἀνάστηθι καὶ στρῶσον σεαυτῷ.

Note the force of the present tense, ἰᾶται, also the fairly full
formula Ἰησοῦς Χριστός (cf. Acts iii. 6; 1 Cor. v. 3-5; and
above, p. 61).

Was Aeneas one of the ἅγιοι of ver. 32? If so, the force of
ἰᾶταί σε Ἰησοῦς Χριστός would be considerable.

IX

LAMENESS

In the passage from Q which contains the message from Jesus to John the Baptist we read that Jesus reminds John that τυφλοὶ ἀναβλέπουσιν καὶ χωλοὶ περιπατοῦσιν, κ.τ λ. (Mt. xi. 5 = Lk. vii. 22), and a passage peculiar to Mt. (xxi. 14) tells us προσῆλθον αὐτῷ τυφλοὶ καὶ χωλοὶ ἐν τῷ ἱερῷ καὶ ἐθεράπευσεν αὐτούς. The Gospels do not, however, provide us with an example of a specific instance in which our Lord heals a person who is described as χωλός. In the Judean section [1] of Acts, on the other hand, there are two cases thus described, one is cured by Peter, the other by Paul.

We shall do well to bear in mind the possible influence of Is. xxxv. 6 (LXX) on the details of these accounts :

$$τότε ἀλεῖται ὡς ἔλαφος ὁ χωλός,$$
$$τρανὴ δὲ ἔσται γλῶσσα μογιλάλων.$$

Healing of the man lame from birth at the 'Beautiful Gate'.

Acts iii. 1–iv. 22.

The account is vivid, and the author describes a cure of a very remarkable kind, for the man is lame from birth (iii. 2), and more than 40 years old (iv. 22). The malady is thought to have its seat in the feet and ankles (iii. 7).

As to the method of cure, note :

Peter and John 'look fixedly' (ἀτενίζειν) at the patient, and Peter tells him to look at them (Βλέψον εἰς ἡμᾶς); the full formula ἐν τῷ ὀνόματι Ἰησοῦ Χριστοῦ τοῦ Ναζωραίου; Peter takes him by the right hand and raises him (cf. Mk. i. 30 f.).

Could the Apostle have adopted a procedure fundamentally more in accord with modern practice ?

[1] See above, p. 29

The cure takes place at once :

παραχρῆμα δὲ ἐστερεώθησαν αἱ βάσεις αὐτοῦ καὶ τὰ σφυρά, καὶ ἐξαλλόμενος ἔστη καὶ περιεπάτει, καὶ εἰσῆλθεν σὺν αὐτοῖς εἰς τὸ ἱερὸν περιπατῶν καὶ ἀλλόμενος [1] καὶ αἰνῶν τὸν θεόν.

It is noteworthy that the narrative again and again emphasizes the fact that Peter performed the cure not by his own power but by that of Jesus Christ (iii. 12, 16 ; iv. 10, 12). Cf. ix. 34.[2]

Healing of man lame from birth at Lystra.

Acts xiv. 8 ff.

There is a striking similarity between this case and that just considered. Ver. 8 describes a severe organic affliction. Paul comes across a man sitting, who was ἀδύνατος τοῖς ποσίν, χωλὸς ἐκ κοιλίας μητρὸς αὐτοῦ, ὃς οὐδέποτε περιεπάτησεν.

As did Peter in the previous instance so here Paul 'looks fixedly' (ἀτενίσας) at the patient. We are reminded of the Synoptic accounts of healing. Paul first sees that the man has faith to be cured (σωθῆναι), and then, μεγάλῃ φωνῇ, he says, Ἀνάστηθι ἐπὶ τοὺς πόδας σου ὀρθός.

Result immediate : ἥλατο [3] καὶ περιεπάτει.

Taking the data provided in these two cases of lameness from birth as being strictly accurate, I am unable to adduce any parallel to them. It is advisable, none the less, not to lose sight of two facts : (1) Doctors who practise psycho-analysis will tell us that patients frequently come to them with a physical disability from which they say they have suffered from birth, and yet subsequent analysis reveals the fact that in reality the malady first attacked them in (for example) their third or fourth year. The patient, be it understood, was genuinely ignorant of this. (2) Lameness from birth is usually due to 'Infantile Paralysis'. It is by no means rare for this

---

[1] Cf. Isa. xxxv. 6 quoted above.

[2] iii. 16 as it stands is clumsy and not consistent with itself. See Prof. C. C. Torrey, op cit , p. 14 ff., who shows that ἐστερέωσεν τὸ ὄνομα αὐτοῦ is probably a mistranslation from the Aramaic, and that Lk. read שְׁמֵהּ הָקֵם, whereas he should have read הָקֵם שְׁמֵהּ = ὑγιῆ ἐποίησεν (or κατέστησεν) αὐτόν, which would be both idiomatic and agreeable to the context.

[3] Cf Isa. xxxv. 6 quoted above.

organic disease to improve as the child grows older, but often, after the organic element in the disease has righted itself, the symptoms continue 'hysterically'; the patient, arguing unconsciously from past experience, thinks that he never will be able to walk properly, and therefore, even though the organic cause of the complaint has vanished (unbeknown to the sufferer), the morbid symptoms are in no way abated, but are sustained by autosuggestion.

It is reasonable for those who wish to do so to suppose that the two cases under consideration may be explained in one or other of the above ways, in which case the illustrations already supplied from modern therapy in respect of paralysis would be equally applicable here.

X

BLINDNESS

The blind man at Bethsaida.   Mk. viii. 22-26.

THIS case and that of the 'deaf stammerer' (Mk. vii. 31-7) are the only two instances in the Synoptic Gospels where we are given a picture of our Lord employing popular medical remedies in the curing of disease.   They are both peculiar to Mk.   But there are no sufficient reasons for believing that these passages are later accretions to Mk.'s gospel, nor need it be supposed that Lk. was not acquainted with them.   The details in them are such that we may well believe that Lk. omitted them purposely, not, perhaps, because he thought them derogatory to our Lord, but at least because he considered them not sufficiently edifying.[1]   The reason for Mt.'s omitting them does not need discussion.   It should, however, be noted that he substitutes the cure of great multitudes for that of the deaf stammerer (Mt. xv. 29-31 = Mk. vii. 31-7), and, from what has been observed elsewhere of his apparent treatment of sources, it is probable that he was aware of the Marcan narrative.[2]

---

[1] Cf. Sir John Hawkins, *O. S. S. P.*, pp. 64-7.
[2] See above, p. 54.

Loisy[1] sees in these two stories indications of Mk.'s symbolism, and maintains that we are justified in laying stress on their allegorical signification only, the details being too doubtful for any conclusions to be drawn from them. I do not think that this view does justice to the simplicity of the accounts.

Account:

φέρουσιν αὐτῷ τυφλόν, καὶ παρακαλοῦσιν αὐτὸν ἵνα αὐτοῦ ἅψηται.

So he took the b'ind man by the hand and led him out of the village. Then, after spitting on his eyes (πτύσας εἰς τὰ ὄμματα αὐτοῦ), he 'laid his hands on him and asked, him if he saw anything

Beginning to see again (ἀναβλέψας),[2] the man said,

βλέπω τοὺς ἀνθρώπους ὅτι ὡς δένδρα ὁρῶ περιπατοῦντας.

At this he laid his hands on his eyes (ἐπὶ τοὺς ὀφθαλμοὺς αὐτοῦ) once more.

καὶ διέβλεψεν καὶ ἀπεκατέστη, καὶ ἐνέβλεπεν τηλαυγῶς ἅπαντα.

Jesus sent him home, saying, Do not go into the village.

It is clear from the story as it is related that the man had not always been blind (ver. 24). Apparently those who brought him thought that it was only necessary for Jesus to touch him in order that he might regain his sight (ver. 22). But Jesus was not a miraculous therapeutic machine: He dealt with individuals individually and personally, and not in a mechanical way. Even when surrounded by a crowd and urgently needed elsewhere He would not allow the woman who had been cured by surreptitiously touching His clothes to go away without a personal conversation (see Mk. v. 25-34 and prls.). And so here He gives up His time and attention to the blind man.

In using saliva during the process of cure our Lord was employing a popular remedy.[3]   The belief in its efficacy may

---

[1] *E. S.*, i. 1007 ff.

[2] See below, p. 105, n. 3

[3] Cf. a similar cure reported to have been worked by Vespasian (Tacitus, *Hist.* iv. 81 ; Suetonius, *Vespas.* 7). Also the passage in the *Satyricon* of Petronius Arbiter, where the tale is told of a witch performing an instant cure by

be traced to animistic ideas. Thus Warneck,[1] writing of beliefs and practices among the Battaks, says : ' Saliva is medicinal, because it contains soul power, and is frequently spread upon the sick. Those who offer sacrifices spit upon the offering in order to add to it a part of themselves. Expectorated saliva must not be allowed to fall into the hands of an enemy.' Again he writes[2] : ' Friendships and covenants are ratified by a mutual drinking of blood, or by the parties mixing some drops of their own blood in order that their souls may be blended. . . . The same consideration makes one like to be spat upon by people who are accounted fortunate. Poor people appropriate the chewed betel leaves of great chiefs and gulp them down in order to bring something of their glory to their own souls. People who are clever at speaking are entreated to spit into one's mouth.'

We may compare the following therapeutic formula from an Assyrian inscription[3] :

'The man of Ea am I, the man of Damkina am I, the messenger of Marduk am I. The great lord Ea hath sent me to revive thee . . . sick man ; he hath added his pure spell to mine, he hath added his pure voice to mine, he hath added his pure spittle to mine, he hath added his pure prayer to mine ; the destroyer(s) of the limbs, which are in the body of the sick man, hath the power to destroy the limbs—by the magic of the word of Ea may these evil ones be put to flight.'

Animistic ideas regarding saliva may be further illustrated from the beliefs and practices of the Masai. Among them

making a cake of clay with her spittle and anointing the patient therewith (ch. 131, quoted by Conybeare, *J. Q. R.*, vol. ix, p. 455). On certain specific curative effects of saliva see Galen, *Nat. Facul.* iii. 7. Cf also the following : ' The battle of Horus with Set, which as we shall see was a Solar incident, waged so fiercely that the young god lost his eye at the hands of his father's enemy. When Set was overthrown, and it was finally recovered by Thoth, this wise god spat upon the wound and healed it This method of healing the eye, which is, of course, folk-medicine reflected in the myth, evidently gained wide popularity, passed into Asia, and seems to reappear in the New Testament narrative, in the incident which depicts Jesus doubtless deferring to recognized folk-custom in employing the same means to heal a blind man ' (J. H. Breasted, *Development of Religion and Thought in Ancient Egypt*, p 31).

[1] Joh Warneck, *The Living Forces of the Gospel*, p 45.
[2] Ibid., p. 54.
[3] Extract from Utukku-series Tablet, III. l. 65 (taken from R. Campbell Thompson, *E. R. E.*, art. ' Disease and Medicine' [Assyro-Babylonian]).

blessing consisted of spitting upon the recipient.[1] It was, however, more common as a vehicle for the curse, or as a symbol of contempt or insult. Therefore the Masai spat while cursing. 'If a man while cursing spits in his enemy's eyes, blindness is supposed to follow.'[2]

What value our Lord attributed to the use of spittle it is impossible to say. Assuming its value was a mental one it does not follow, even if He did not appreciate this, that He held animistic beliefs about it such as those discussed above. Ordinary people who are not doctors even in these enlightened times take medicines and apply remedies because they seem to work, but they rarely understand their *modus operandi*. We do not on that account accuse them of erroneous opinions regarding the working of these things. Such people do not bother themselves about the way in which they operate. It is by no means impossible that Jesus took a similar line with regard to the medicaments of His day.

It is necessary to bear in mind that, in spite of the relatively numerous records of healing in the Gospels, the information provided respecting our Lord's methods is very fragmentary. These instances peculiar to Mk. where the use of saliva is recorded belong, in my opinion, to a very early stratum of the Gospel records. As has already been noted frequently, Mk. usually gives us a more natural description of the cures than the other Synoptists, while in the latter there is an unmistakable tendency to 'heighten' the miracle (though this tendency is sometimes exaggerated by critics). A good example of this process of heightening is to be observed in the case of Peter's mother-in-law (Mk. i. 29-31 and prls.).[3] By 'heightening' I mean a stressing of the marvellous element in the healing with a consequent blurring of the true perspective in which to view the historical event. This tendency seems to me the most probable reason for the omission by Mt. and Lk. of the two cases in Mk. where spittle is employed. It is, then, a reasonable inference that our Lord used popular remedies as constituent parts of His cures much more often than is generally

---

[1] J. Thomson, *Through Masai Land*, p. 165 fl. (London, 1887), quoted by A. E. Crawley, *E R E*, art 'Cursing and Blessing'.

[2] S. L. and H. Hinde, *Last of the Masai*, p. 48 (1901), quoted by Crawley, ibid.

[3] See above, p 81 f

supposed. In this connexion it is instructive to note that it is only Mk. in the accounts of the mission of the Twelve who records their practice of anointing the sick with oil (Mk. vi. 13).[1] Perhaps Jesus sometimes employed this remedy also.

Mk. x. 46–52 ; Lk. xviii. 35–43 ; [Mt. xx. 29-34].

Blind Bartimaeus (name only in Mk.).

Enough has been said in dealing with other miracles recorded in the Synoptics to allow us to take Mk. as our best source in this instance without going minutely into the arguments which justify us in so doing. As a matter of fact Lk. follows Mk. practically word for word in all important particulars except one (which will be noted). Mt. quite clearly obtains his two blind men by combining this case with that of the blind man of Bethsaida (cf. Mt. xx. 34 with Mk. viii. 23).[2]

The narrative obviously indicates that the patient had not always been blind. His petition is that he may regain (ἀνα-βλέπω)[3] his sight. But further, Mk. (as opposed to Lk.) hints that he was not totally blind. A comparison between Mk. and Lk. on this point is very instructive. Lk. omits the details in Mk., verses 49 b and 50, which are as follows: Jesus stopped, and said, ' Call him. Then they called the blind man, saying to him, Take courage ! Get up, he is calling you. Throwing off his cloak he jumped up and went to Jesus (ἀναπηδήσας ἦλθεν πρὸς τὸν Ἰησοῦν).' For this Lk. substitutes : Jesus ' ordered him to be brought (ἀχθῆναι) to him. And when he approached he asked him,' &c.

The Marcan account suggests that the man came to Jesus unaided. It cannot be denied that he might conceivably have

---

[1] A practice which has probably never been entirely abandoned by the Church (cf. James v. 13-16; Tertullian, *Ad Scapulam*, 4, &c.). It is worth observing that the practice of anointing with oil seems to have had its roots in primitive animistic beliefs, and to be the outcome of the same idea which led to the employment of spittle (cf. Dr. Buchanan Gray, *E. B.*, 175).

[2] Cf. above, p. 54.

[3] This seems to be undoubtedly the meaning of the word here. Cf. the extract in Moulton and Milligan, *The Vocab. of the Greek Test*, from an inscription about a blind man ' recovering sight ' in the temple of Asclepios : καὶ ἀνέβλεψεν καὶ ἐλήλυθεν καὶ ηὐχαρίστησεν δημοσίᾳ τῷ θεῷ (*Sylloge Inscriptionum Graecarum*, 807[11] [ii/A.D.], ed. W. Dittenberger).

been able to do this if he was totally blind. It is, however, quite a reasonable inference that he was able to see a little, even if only very faintly. Manifestly Lk. has corrected what he probably took to be a mere ambiguity on the part of Mk. But we know enough of Lk. to be fairly sure that he would, in a case of doubt, be inclined to exaggerate rather than minimize the marvellous, and therefore we cannot attach much evidential value to his correction here.

The remaining points to note for our purpose are :

(1) the man's persistence (Mk. ver. 48 and prls.);
(2) an immediate cure follows the words of Jesus, ὕπαγε, ἡ πίστις σου σέσωκέν σε (Mk. ver. 52).[1]

I omit a discussion of Mt.'s 'blind and dumb demoniac', since we are only provided with the general statement that he was healed, and also because the evidence for the meagre facts related is not of a very high order.

St. Paul's blindness.

There are three accounts in Acts of Paul's conversion. The first and most detailed (ix. 1-19) occurs in the ' Judean section '. The other two purport to be described by Paul himself, one in a speech to the Jews in Jerusalem (xxii. 4-16), the other in his speech before Agrippa (xxvi. 9-20), both occurring in the latter half of the book. They are all agreed in affirming that on the road to Damascus Paul had a dazzling and overpowering vision of light which caused him to fall to the ground ; that he heard a voice saying to him, Saul, Saul, why dost thou persecute me ? ; and that, on his asking who spoke to him, the reply came, I am Jesus whom thou persecutest.

That Paul's conversion was marked by a crisis in which he had a vision of the Lord it seems impossible to doubt, especially in view of the corroborating evidence of his own affirmations in Gal. i. 15, 16; 1 Cor. ix. 1 ; and 1 Cor. xv. 5-8. With regard to the minor details of the scene of the vision the evidence is, to some extent, conflicting, but this perhaps

---

[1] Lk.'s ἀνάβλεψον for Mk.'s ὕπαγε is probably due to the fact that the writer did not like to represent the blind man as being disobedient to Jesus's command by following Him (vid. καὶ ἠκολούθει αὐτῷ). I do not think it necessary to enter into the questions raised by the use of the title 'Son of David' (see Foakes Jackson and Lake, *B. Chr.*, p. 365 f., and Dalman, op. cit., p. 319 ff.).

strengthens rather than otherwise the evidence for the main features of the story.[1]

Paul, in his speech before Agrippa, does not mention his blindness subsequent to the vision, and the cure by Ananias, nor is there any reference to this in his epistles. It is not therefore surprising that it has frequently been held, especially at a period less alive than the present day to the occurrence of abnormal mental and spiritual phenomena, that the narratives under consideration are a translation into the language of history of the figurative expressions of the manifestation of Christ to Paul's soul and the consequent change from spiritual darkness to light (cf. Baur, ' Paul ', *E. T.* 1[76]; Zeller, 'Acts ', *E. T.* 1[299]).[2] As regards the account of the blindness and cure this is certainly a legitimate point of view, although, for my own part, I think that the evidence is stronger for the view that we are dealing here with the sub-stance of an historical fact. The blindness and healing by Ananias are described in both of the two main divisions of the book of Acts, and the inconsistencies which are apparent between these two records are of a kind which enhance rather than detract from the likelihood of the historicity of the main facts. Moreover, the relation of these facts in the speech before Agrippa would have been quite superfluous and out of place, and there is no particular reason why mention should have been made of them in any of the Epistles. Hence we can argue nothing from the silence about them in these places.

On these grounds, therefore, I believe that the following facts at least are historical :

> That the immediate result of the crisis on the road to Damascus was that Paul became temporarily blind, that he had on this account to be led to his destination, and that his cure was brought about through the instrumen-tality of a follower of Christ named Ananias.[3]

This is not the place to enter into a lengthy discussion of the psychology of Paul's conversion. It must suffice for me

[1] Cf. Langlois and Seignobos, *Introduction to the Study of History*, p. 201.
[2] See Edwin Hatch, *E. B.* 3608 f.
[3] I do not myself wish to deny the likelihood of the substantial accuracy of the details in Acts ix. 10-19.

to say briefly that, in my opinion, the form in which the
conversion took place was dependent upon the Apostle's
temperament. All the evidence of his characteristics points
to a temperament to which nowadays we should probably
apply the epithet ' neurotic ' (the word being employed, it should
be made clear, in a technical and not in a disparaging sense).[1]

In addition to many less outstanding features which indicate this conclusion we may note in particular his vehement
and bigoted persecuting zeal prior to his conversion and his
no less vehement enthusiasm after that event. In conjunction
with this we must place the references to his visions and
various ecstatic experiences. Cf., e. g., 2 Cor. xii. 1–12 ;
1 Cor. xiv. 1–19.   See also 2 Cor. x. 10, 11 ; Gal. iv. 13, 14.

I take the view, then, that the blindness which was the outcome of the vision was ' hysterical ' (employing this
word again in a technical sense without any disparaging connotation)[2] ; that is to say, that no organic change in the mechanism
of Paul's eyes took place as the result of an objective light of
excessive vividness affecting the retina, but that the blindness
was brought about by purely mental processes.[3]

---

[1] Cf. Prof. H. A. A. Kennedy, *St. Paul and the Mystery-Religions*, p. 286 f.
Dr. Kennedy discusses the similarity between Paul's temperament and that of
the mystics. In speaking of Paul as ' neurotic' I am far from intending to
underrate the fundamental sanity of his outlook. Cf. e.g. his discussion of
spiritual χαρίσματα in 1 Cor. xii-xiv.   Oskar Pfister, *The Psychoanalytic
Method*, p. 576 f., maintains that in Jesus we find ' the piety of the healthiest
and most profound thinker of men ', while Paul represents 'the piety of the
neurotic'. See also Pfister, op. cit., p. 462 f.

[2] Cf. the case of the girl ' S. W.', described by Jung, who was ' hysterically
blind ' for half an hour after one of the ecstasies into which she frequently went
(*Analytical Psychology*, p. 21).

[3] It should be noted that, even if it is maintained that the blindness was due
in the first instance to an objective light (cf. Acts xxii. 9, with which contrast
Acts ix. 7), it does not follow that the prolongation of the inability to see until
the visit of Ananias was not the result of autosuggestion.   There is plenty of
evidence that blindness (and, indeed, most other disabilities) initiated by physical causes may be continued unduly, and perhaps indefinitely, by autosuggestion or heterosuggestion, thus becoming ' hysterical '.   This has frequently
been noticed in the recent war where men have temporarily lost their sight from
the effects of poison gas, and the state has continued unnecessarily owing to the
belief that they would never see again (cf. Drs. A. F. Hurst and C. H.
Kipman, *S. H. N. S.*, p. 145 ff.).

Summary of cases of blindness.

In the cases we have been considering the fact emerges that there is every reason to believe that none of the sufferers had always been blind, that is to say, we must take into account the possibility that their disability was 'functional'. With regard to the Apostle Paul's blindness this is, indeed, to my mind, a practical certainty.

In the *Hibbert Journal* of April 1907 (p. 582) Dr. R. J. Ryle wrote : ' There is an affection which is mentioned in books upon diseases of the eye which goes by the name of "hysterical amblyopia", and which is generally found in young people, and these almost always of the female sex. It need hardly be observed that in Syria, as also elsewhere, other causes of blindness are vastly more common, and in both the instances which are recorded in St. Mark's gospel the patients are of the male sex and not young.'

It is not my purpose in the present essay to attempt to support the thesis that all the patients whom our Lord or His followers cured were suffering from maladies which were 'hysterical' or 'functional'. Such a view I consider most unconvincing. On the other hand, it seems to me that recent investigations have made it plain that the particular instances of blindness with which we are immediately concerned were quite probably of a 'functional' nature. To confine 'hysterical amblyopia' almost exclusively to women and children, as did, for example, Dr. Ryle, is to have gone no further than the limited and one-sided evidence of the school of Charcot at the Salpêtrière. Nowadays investigators are coming to gain some insight into the remarkable part which autosuggestion often plays in the progress of diseases, and to observe its action not merely in women and children and such others as are contemptuously labelled 'hysterics', but amongst all sorts and conditions of men.

The most accessible medically authenticated evidence for functional blindness cured by psychotherapy relates to soldiers who became blind in the late war as the result of shell-concussion or gassing. It is, however, very necessary to bear in mind that in such cases the explosion, mustard gas, or whatever it was, was merely the determining physical occasion which conditioned the subsequent blindness, there was nothing in the explosion, &c., *per se*, which necessitated this result. Thus these instances throw light on a mechanism in human beings which can scarcely be regarded as coming into play solely under war conditions. The numerous cases of functional blindness resulting from the effects of poison gas suggest that a violent concussion is not a necessary factor for the setting in motion of this mechanism. Indeed it seems abundantly clear that all that is necessary to make this possible is some physical (or psychical) misadventure which 'suggests' to the patient that he is, or is becoming, blind. Whether or not he accepts this 'suggestion' will depend upon the degree of his 'suggestibility' at the time, which will in turn depend upon a number of factors, such as, for example, his normal mental characteristics and the particular emotional conditions in which he is placed at the moment. No doubt the emotional state resulting from the strain of active service at the front tends to increase this 'suggestibility', and hence are found the great number of functional complaints brought about in this way; but the stresses and strains of peace time are also potent in inducing the requisite emotional conditions.

When Paul caused the sorcerer Elymas to become blind by hurling his curse of blindness at him (Acts xiii. 6–12) he was doubtless (if the incident be historical) putting into motion just this mechanism of which we have been speaking. In this instance it is the Apostle's word which is the determinant which leads to the blindness, whereas in the case of the soldiers we have been considering it is, as a rule, some physical 'suggestion'; but in either case the lack of sight is really due to the patient himself who has accepted the auto-suggestion of blindness.[1] It may be remarked in passing that the record in Acts leaves us in no doubt as to the intensity of the emotional atmosphere in which the curse of blindness was received.

The foregoing theory of the mechanism which induces hysterical blindness would not be subscribed to by all schools of psychotherapy at the present day. I state it as appearing to me the most adequate to all the facts.

I subjoin an extract from a discussion on hysterical blindness by Drs. A. F. Hurst and A. Wilson Gill,[2] which corroborates

---

[1] It need hardly be said that blindness can be induced in hypnosis. Cf. e. g Albert Moll, *Hypnotism*, p 98 f.

[2] *S. H N. S.*, vol. 1, No. 6, p. 298 ff.

much of what has been said whilst diverging in some particulars, and I also add one of their case reports (as representing many similar ones):

'... Any condition which has led to complete though temporary blindness may suggest to the individual that he has lost his sight for ever : this is particularly likely to be the case if the temporary blindness was produced suddenly under terrifying conditions, as, for example, by the explosion of a powerful shell in the immediate neighbourhood. The slower onset of the temporary blindness in gassing, although the surrounding conditions might be equally terrifying, generally resulted in less profound hysterical blindness. When the suggestion that the sight is permanently lost has become thoroughly accepted, the individual will cease to look. The visual tract is no longer prepared for sight by attention, and visual impulses consequently cease to pass up to the brain. In the act of looking the resistance at each cell-station in the tract is diminished by some process such as a throwing out of dendrites or an alteration in the electro-chemical condition at the synapses. Consequently visual impulses will now not only give rise to no visual perception, but the flinch reflex, which is a mid-brain reflex, and in the most severe cases even the pupil reflex to light, will disappear, as the resistance to the impulse even at the lowest synapsis is too great to be overcome. ... When, as a result of psychotherapy, the patient realizes that he can really see if only he chooses to look, he once more throws out the dendrites (or otherwise reduces the resistance) in the visual path, and vision returns, the pupil and blink reflexes becoming normal again at the same moment. Injury or disease of the visual centre in the occipital cortex is the only organic condition leading to blindness in which the lower visual centres are unaffected. It might consequently be thought that the flinch reflex, which Sherrington has shown is a function of the mid-brain, as it persists after the removal of the cortex in animals, would remain unaltered. It is, however, always lost in the blind fields of vision. The only possible explanation is that the patient, realizing that he is blind in a certain field, ceases to look in this direction ; the dendrites are retracted at the synapses of the affected tracts, and the reflexes consequently disappear. If now the pathological condition of the occipital lobe so improves that vision should again be possible, spontaneous improvement does not necessarily occur. Only if the patient is encouraged to look does he suddenly discover that his field of vision has increased in size, and simultaneously the flinch reflex returns. It is clear from what has been said that in the absence of any abnormality in the eyes there is no means of determining with certainty whether absolute blindness in the whole fields or in homonymous areas is organic or hysterical, as the flinch reflex is lost and the pupil reflex may be sluggish or even absent in both. . . . With the afferent element set in readiness, visual impulses reach the occipital lobes, but nothing is seen clearly until the eyes are opened, the external muscles work in thorough co-ordination so that the object to be looked at is brought into the centre of both the fields, and the ciliary muscles contract just sufficiently to bring it into correct focus. All these motor processes may be impaired as a result of suggestion, either alone, as in the slighter cases of hysterical disturbance of vision which occurred so frequently after gassing, or in addition to the afferent element already considered. . . . [Here follows an account of different kinds of motor disorder.] . . . These various motor abnormalities may be present in any combination. They all require the same treatment—psychotherapy—explanation, re-education in looking and persuasion being sufficient in almost every instance to produce a rapid cure.'

Case Report.[1] Total blindness with loss of pupil reflexes following shell-concussion :

'Pnr. B., aged 41, went to France in September, 1914. After six weeks' fighting he was stunned as the result of the explosion of a shell in his immediate vicinity. In the evening he noticed he could not see clearly and attributed this to the shock of the explosion. He at once thought he would lose his sight : his eyelids began to droop and he had difficulty in focussing objects. He was sent to England, where the use of various eye-drops and dark glasses confirmed his fears, and in a short time he became totally blind. Early in 1915 he was discharged as permanently unfit, receiving a pension of twenty-five shillings a week. He was examined every six

[1] Op. cit , p. 302 f.

months after this, but no treatment was given. An operation was advised but refused by the patient, as the surgeon would not promise a cure. A diagnosis of choroiditis was made on one occasion. In November, 1918, he was seen by Mr. J. R. Rolston, of Plymouth, who recognized the condition as hysterical and advised his transfer to Seale Hayne Hospital, where he was admitted on November 13, 1918. He now presented the picture of the typical blind beggar of the street. Unshaven, unkempt, and dirty, and wearing a pair of dark glasses, he came supported by his wife, while in his hand he carried a thick stick to guide himself along the streets. Whilst wearing the glasses he could open his eyelids freely, but could see nothing, but when they were removed he was unable to open the lids owing to severe blepharospasm, except in a darkened room or in the dusk. Treatment was commenced the same evening, and in a short time the patient overcame the blepharospasm and opened his eyes, but he was still totally blind. The pupils were then found widely dilated, with no trace of reaction to light. The flinch reflex was completely absent in both eyes. Ophthalmoscopic examination showed nothing abnormal, and a definite diagnosis of hysterical blindness was made. Explanation as to the nature of his condition and encouragement to use his eyes rapidly led to partial restoration of his vision, but at the end of two hours he still stumbled over objects placed in his path. After a rest of an hour, treatment was continued and further slight improvement occurred. In attempting to focus he made strong contractions of the muscles of the neck and rotated the head towards the left side. He could see nothing if he looked straight at the object. The contractions of the neck muscles were similar to those seen in the spastic variety of aphonia when the patient attempts to speak, being simply due to mis-directed effort. The next morning he was taken out of doors and distant objects were soon recognized. An endeavour was then made to teach him to focus his eyes on nearer objects, and by the evening he could read 6/24 at 20 feet. The excessive contractions of the neck muscles continued, however, but, by encouraging him to relax and to depend entirely on his eyes, vision steadily improved. He was still inclined to stumble over objects placed in his path, but this was merely due to inattention. On November 25 he could read with each eye in turn 6/12 at 20 feet and could spell words printed in small type, but as he was almost completely illiterate he could not pronounce them. The flinch reflex and the normal pupillary reactions to light had returned the first evening. Anaesthesia of the cornea, which was present at first, was proved to be due to inattention, and immediately disappeared on his attention being drawn to the fact. The patient was also completely deaf in the left ear on admission ; he was given instruction in listening, and at the end of a week he could hear normally When seen four months later, in February 1919, he was at work as a watchmaker and gramophone repairer, and could both see and hear quite well.'

Attention should be drawn to the fact that the patient in the above case had been blind for four years.

The illustrations I have given have been in the realm of 'hysterical' blindness. But, in addition, we must not leave out of account that there is evidence (and that of a kind not lightly to be rejected) that psychotherapy has cured organic diseases of the eye.[1]

XI

'DEAF STAMMERER'

Mk. vii. 31–37.

> καὶ φέρουσιν αὐτῷ κωφὸν καὶ μογιλάλον καὶ παρακαλοῦσιν αὐτὸν
> ἵνα ἐπιθῇ αυτῷ τὴν χεῖρα

On the value of the source and the method of cure adopted see the discussion of the 'blind man at Bethsaida' (above, p. 101 ff.).

It is not sufficiently profitable for the purpose in hand to discuss Mk.'s much debated 'itinerary' at this point of the narrative. (See, e.g., Loisy, *E. S.*, i. 978 ff; Burkitt, *G. H. T.*, p. 92 ff.)

---

[1] See the detailed (and illustrated) account of two cures of corneal ulcer by Dr. Bonjour of Lausanne (*Les Guérisons miraculeuses modernes*, p 31 ff.).

Loisy [1] maintains that μογιλάλος should not be translated in its etymological sense of 'stammerer', but that it follows its use in Isa. xxxv. 6 (LXX) where it translates the Hebrew אִלֵּם, which means 'dumb'. But the words 'he began to speak correctly' (καὶ ἐλάλει ὀρθῶς) at the end of ver. 35 tell strongly against this view ; [2] and we need not attach great importance to the words ἀλάλους λαλεῖν (37) attributed to the astonished folk who were informed of the miracle.

The preservation of the Aramaic word ἐφφαθά (= ? אֶתְפְּתַח) seems to indicate that it was believed in itself to possess peculiar potency — an idea common enough in primitive thought.[3] (Cf. Mk. v. 41.) On ὁ δεσμὸς τῆς γλώσσης (35) see Adolf Deissmann, *Light from the Ancient East*, p. 306 ff, who claims that it is a technical expression taken from magic. After citing many examples, he says : 'From these and many other texts we see what the ancients thought of as the result of binding the tongue, viz. inability to speak. The man whose tongue was bound was intended to become thereby dumb, so we may conclude conversely that the tongue of a dumb person was often considered in ancient popular belief to have been "bound" by some daemon. This view fits in with the wider complex of widespread ancient beliefs that certain diseases and morbid conditions were caused in general by daemonic possession. Jesus Himself says (Lk. xiii. 16) that Satan had "bound" a daughter of Abraham eighteen years. He means the crooked woman previously mentioned in the context, "which had a spirit of infirmity", and whose "bond" was loosed on the Sabbath. It seems probable, therefore, that St. Mark's "bond of his tongue" is also a technical expression. The writer will not merely say that a dumb man was made to speak—he will add further that daemonic fetters were broken, a work of Satan undone.' [4]   Cf. Mt. ix. 32, 33 a : ἰδοὺ προσ-

---

[1] *E. S.*, ad loc.

[2] Cf. Lagrange, *Saint Marc*, p 187.   He notes the number of critics who hold μογιλάλος here to be equivalent to אִלֵּם, and says, 'Mais à supposer que Mc. ait eu en vue le passage d'Isaïe, rien ne prouve qu'il ait vérifie le texte hébreu ; le grec τρανὴ δὲ ἔσται γλῶσσα μογιλάλων suggérait plutôt le sens de " parlant d'une voix confuse ".'

[3] Cf. A. E. Crawley, art, 'Cursing and Blessing', *E. R. E.*

[4] I do not think that this argument conclusively supports the view of those who contend that the patient in the present instance was completely dumb.

ἤνεγκαν αὐτῷ ἄνθρωπον κωφὸν δαιμονιζόμενον· καὶ ἐκβληθέντος τοῦ δαιμονίου ἐλάλησεν ὁ κωφός. The narrative tells us that, after Jesus had put His fingers into the man's ears and, spitting, had touched his tongue, ἀναβλέψας εἰς τὸν οὐρανὸν ἐστέναξεν. It is a valuable reminder of how human and non-magical the actual scene was.

The patient's right speech returned directly his ears were 'opened' (ver. 35).

In modern practice it is admitted that deafness and disabilities of speech are symptoms which may be 'hysterical', in the sense of being initiated by suggestion and curable by psychotherapy. Deafness and mutism (of varying degrees of completeness) are comparatively often associated together.[1] Dr. A. F. Hurst says that 'hysterical deafness is probably less rare in civil life than has generally been supposed'.[2] It is interesting to note that he maintains that 'when hysterical deafness is associated with mutism it requires no special treatment, as hearing almost invariably returns spontaneously when speech is restored'.[3] We find the converse of this in Mk. vii. 35 (καὶ ἠνοίγησαν αὐτοῦ αἱ ἀκοαί, καὶ εὐθὺς ἐλύθη ὁ δεσμὸς τῆς γλώσσης αὐτοῦ, κ. τ. λ.).

Stammering Dr. J. F. Venables holds to be 'invariably an hysterical symptom'.[4] This statement, he says, may at first appear to be exaggerated ; 'it certainly would be dangerous if it led to the idea that in all cases of stammering it was only necessary to treat the hysterical symptom and remove it by rapid methods, either by re-education or gross suggestion, in order to cure the individual of his disability. The statement must be modified by saying that, although stammering is always an hysterical symptom, and in many cases is an hysterical symptom in an otherwise normal individual, in other cases it is only a symptom of minor importance, except in so far as it points to an underlying condition of moderate or

---

[1] e g. this association is found in 4 out of 10 cases of mutism cited by Dr. M. D. Eder (*War-Shock*, p. 28).

[2] See ' The causes, diagnosis, and treatment of hysterical deafness, with notes on the auditory-motor reflex and the psychology of hearing ', *S H. N. S*, vol 1, No. 5, p. 279 ff. Dr. Hurst uses the word ' hysterical ' in the sense defined above.

[3] Ibid., p. 288.

[4] *S. H. N. S.*, vol. i, No. 6, p. 333.

severe psychasthenia'.[1] Dr. Venables gives reasons for this theory, and states that his practice with soldiers helped to confirm it. 'Directly treatment was commenced on the assumption that the condition was hysterical and therefore rapidly curable, much better results were at once obtained, as was only to be expected if the theory was correct.'[2] In many cases a bad stammerer was speaking quite normally at the end of one treatment.[3] This view, however, is not one which has been, up till now, generally held, as will be seen from the following report, quoted by Dr. Venables,[4] of the words of the President of the Laryngological Section of the Royal Society of Medicine at a discussion in 1918 : ' With regard to stammering he had nothing favourable to say. The results of treatment had been very unsatisfactory, and the only possible course seemed to be to discharge the stammering soldier from the Army.'[5]

The following are two of Dr.Venables'cases. It will be noticed that the second practically might be described as a 'civilian' case.

(1) 'Stammer dating from childhood, associated with aphonia, cured by psychotherapy :

Pte. S. was admitted suffering from aphonia of seven months' duration following gassing. He was treated the following day in the presence of a class of eight medical officers, and at the end of a few minutes was phonating normally. When told to repeat his name and number he commenced to stammer badly. . . . He was told at once that now that his voice had returned there was no reason at all for him to stammer ; he replied, however, that he had stammered " all his life ". Treatment was at once commenced for the stammer, and within half an hour he was talking with no difficulty at all. He remained quite normal for the remaining four weeks he was in hospital, and never exhibited a trace of hesitation. Inquiry showed that he had stammered since falling off a bicycle at the age of eleven. This case responded to treatment with unusual ease, owing to the fact that the patient was much

---

[1] *S. H. N S*, vol. i, No. 6, p. 333.   [2] Ibid , p. 336.
[3] It was sometimes necessary to continue a sitting for as long as four hours (ibid., p. 340)
[4] Ibid., p. 336.
[5] Cf. Dr. Eder, *War-Shock*, p. 31, who found in his practice that stammering was less easy to cure than the apparently more serious speech defects.

impressed by the return of his voice after his long period of aphonia, and was in consequence ready to believe that his other disability would be removed with equal rapidity.'[1]

(2) 'Stammer following spontaneous disappearance of aphonia:

Pte. S. had developed aphonia through "laryngitis" contracted while dealing with dirty dressings at a base hospital; a sister had gone off duty a few days previously through aphonia supposed to be contracted in the same way, so the exciting cause of his aphonia was probably subconscious imitation. The aphonia persisted for a long time and he subsequently stammered. On admission he had been stammering many months. He was treated as a purely hysterical case and regained his normal speech in the course of forty-eight hours.'[2]

Dr. M. D. Eder holds that deaf mutism may sometimes be a wish-fulfilment. This was so, he maintains, in the following case of a soldier, aged 25, who was cured by him:[3]

'No. 36 was in the trenches with a mate with whom he had enlisted in Australia; this friend of many years' standing was killed by a machine-gun fired a yard in front of him. He lost his head that day and felt unbalanced. He felt he must get outside the trenches and climbed on to the parapet, whence he was pulled back by the sergeant several times. Two days later, after a shell explosion a yard away, by which he was partially buried, he lost consciousness. He recovered some days later to find himself on board ship; he could neither speak nor hear and could hardly stand on his legs. Under hypnosis he could recall whispering a few words as he was being carried on board and had then again relapsed into unconsciousness. The wish for death can be gathered from this history; the attempt to climb on to the parapet which was described by himself as suicidal; the relapse into loss of consciousness (taking the original loss of consciousness as due to *commotio cerebri*); the inability to stand; the deaf mutism which outlasts the other symptoms as the wish for death weakens, death which severs communication between man and his fellows and is well symbolised by deafness and

---

[1] *S H. N. S*, vol. 1, No. 6, p. 336 f.   The last sentence shows an interesting parallel with the N. T. case we are considering.
[2] Ibid., p. 337.
[3] *War-Shock*, pp. 70 f. and 149.

speechlessness.   Sometimes mutism by itself is the symbol of
this wish for death, to have done with the horrors of the battlefield.   It will be gathered that this is quite consistent with
bravery in the battlefield or in the trenches, each representing
partial elements in the man's mental make-up.   Of course, if
any investigator were stupid enough to ask such patients did
they want to die, they would properly answer no ; they might
even say that they had never thought of it, although closer
investigation will not infrequently show such a thought had
been present, though perhaps but fleetingly.   Clearly the
wish for death is incomplete ; they do not die, they only more
or less simulate death.'

The following account by Dr. Wilson Gill respecting the
treatment of soldiers suffering from 'hysterical aphonia' is of
special interest as indicating the conditions found desirable in
order to affect a cure--conditions in essence similar to those
which apparently obtained in the Marcan case with which we
are immediately concerned.

'On admission the medical officer interviews the patient and
obtains his history.   He then definitely promises a cure as
soon as he can find time to give the necessary treatment.   In
the short interval of waiting the patient comes across several
other men who had been admitted shortly before and who
were rapidly cured, so that, as a rule, by the time the medical
officer is ready the patient is ready to be cured.'[1]   'The
treatment is . . . by direct persuasion, but it is often advisable
to perform simultaneously gentle manipulations with the
fingers over the glottis, giving verbal encouragement and
persuasion all the time.   The cure is almost invariably complete in anything from half a minute to one hour.   Delay is
usually the fault of the medical officer and not the fault of the
patient.   It is necessary, therefore, not to lose one's temper.
If fatigued or unfit, the medical officer will find it better to
delay treatment until a more suitable occasion arises, as
temporary failure tends to make one less confident in the
treatment, and vice versa success in treatment increases one's
confidence and ensures rapid results.   Recently three of us
attempted to cure four cases of aphonia in another hospital
after a long, cold, and tiring night journey.   We failed in all

[1] *S. H. N. S.*, vol. i, No. 3, p. 157.

four cases after a full hour. On admission to Seale Hayne Military Hospital some days later, all four cases were cured within an hour at the first attempt.'[1]

For cases unconnected with war of disabilities of speech and hearing amenable to psychotherapy see, e.g., on stammering, Wetterstrand, *Hypnotism and its Application to Practical Medicine* [E.T. 1897], p. 36 ff, and Bjerre, *The History and Practice of Psychanalysis* | E.T. 1916] p. 148 ff;[2] on aphonia and mutism, Dubois, *The Psychic Treatment of Nervous Disorders* [E.T. 6th ed, 1909] p. 314 ff.;[3] on 'hysterical deafness', Pfister, *The Psychoanalytic Method* [1913, E.T. 1917], p. 96 f. Prof. Charles Baudouin gives the case of a girl, aged 7, who as the result of typhoid when 14 months old was totally deaf and able to produce 'nothing but inarticulate sounds'. The speech difficulty was remedied. It is not, however, clear from Baudouin's account whether or not the deafness was affected.[4]

XII

WOMAN WITH A HAEMORRHAGE -

Mk. v. 25-34 ; Lk. viii. 43-48 ; Mt. ix. 20-22.

Mk. καὶ γυνὴ οὖσα ἐν ῥύσει αἵματος δώδεκα ἔτη
Lk. καὶ γυνὴ οὖσα ἐν ῥύσει αἵματος ἀπὸ ἐτῶν δώδεκα
Mt. καὶ ἰδοὺ γυνὴ αἱμορροοῦσα δώδεκα ἔτη

Mk. gives us the fullest account of this incident. There are few narratives in the Gospels which bear such marks of

---

[1] *S. H. N. S* , vol. 1, No. 3, p 158

[2] The case here recorded is not exactly one of stammering; the writer says that it would often happen that 'suddenly without the slightest warning the patient's tongue refused to do its work '.

[3] Dubois says that 'aphonia, like mutism, occurs always as the result of an autosuggestion of helplessness, whether it follows a movement of conscious or subconscious timidity, or whether it has for its starting-point a fortuitous trouble of phonation. Hoarseness, occasioned by a cold or by the inhalation of gas or dust, is enough to give rise to the mental representation of helplessness ' (p. 315). Again, 'All physicians can cure these patients, and all means are good if they suggest the conviction of cure ' (ibid.).

[4] *Suggestion and Autosuggestion* (E. T. 1920) p. 234 f.

historical accuracy as does this record. It is psychologically thoroughly convincing. Incidentally it throws a flood of light upon our Lord's character and His attitude to the Law, for the woman was virtually unclean (see Lev. xv. 25) and, after she had touched Him, technically He was unclean too (ibid. ver. 27).

It is not likely that Lk. and Mt. employed a source other than Mk. here. The addition of προσελθοῦσα and τοῦ κρασπέδου in Lk. viii. 44 a (= Mt. ix. 20 b) is not strong evidence to the contrary.[1] The words τοῦ κρασπέδου may be a reminiscence of Mk. vi. 56.

The following are the elements in the story which require attention :

(1) The malady. It is more probable than not that this was what is now called menorrhagia. The woman had suffered from this for a long time—Mk. says twelve years.[2] She had spent her all on physicians in the endeavour to be cured. This is natural enough when the levitical laws concerning impurity are remembered. We obtain a glimpse here on the one hand into her desperation of mind owing to her condition and failure to find a remedy, and on the other into the faith which must have been hers to enable her to take the risk of the consequences of breaking a sacred convention and wilfully coming into contact with her fellow men.

(2) She came up behind Jesus and touched His clothes, thinking that would be sufficient to bring about a cure.

(3) Result : εὐθὺς ἐξηράνθη ἡ πηγὴ τοῦ αἵματος αὐτῆς, καὶ ἔγνω τῷ σώματι ὅτι ἴαται ἀπὸ τῆς μάστιγος.

(4) Jesus 'at once became aware of the power that had gone out of him ',[3] and insisted on finding out who had touched Him.

---

[1] Cf. Burkitt. *G. H. T.*, p. 441.

[2] We cannot insist on the accuracy of this detail. Cf. ver. 42. Is it a coincidence that Jairus's daughter was twelve years old !

[3] This is an interesting detail, and one not lightly to be dismissed as an accretion reflecting later Christological theories. If the account had been intended to manifest our Lord's supernatural knowledge it is hardly probable that it would have described at length His efforts to find out who the healed person was. The expression ' the power that had gone out from him ' may be metaphorical, but at least it implies a conscious apprehension of a psychical contact between Him and an unknown patient. If we admit (as I think we must) that Jesus was supremely sensitive, and if we take into account the woman's obvious concen-

(5) Ἡ δὲ γυνὴ φοβηθεῖσα καὶ τρέμουσα, εἰδυῖα ὃ γέγονεν αὐτῇ, ἦλθεν καὶ προσέπεσεν αὐτῷ καὶ εἶπεν αὐτῷ πᾶσαν τὴν ἀλήθειαν.[1] We need again to remind ourselves of the enormity of the crime she had committed in coming through the crowd and touching Jesus.

(6) Our Lord treats her gently, calling her 'daughter', and tells her that it is her faith which has brought about her cure. (Is this not what a modern doctor would have said if he had witnessed the scene?) Finally He tells her to go in peace, and to be free of the 'scourge' which has afflicted her. Psychologists would say that He thus saved her from a morbid 'complex' arising out of her illegal act, and so very likely from another disease or the recurrence of her old one.

Maladies akin to that which we must suppose afflicted the woman in this story frequently have been cured by mental treatment. Dr. J. Bonjour of Lausanne says, 'Les exemples de lactation et d'hémorragies taries par l'émotion ne sont pas rares chez la femme; j'en observe des cas chaque année. L'émotion interrompt la grossesse. Tous ces faits sont faciles à contrôler'.[2] August Forel (to take another author) bears ample testimony to the success of psychotherapy in this domain. Thus he writes: 'The most extraordinary phenomena of suggestion are found in the vasomotor, secretory, and exudative actions. One can produce menstruation in women by simple prophesying during hypnosis, or can cause it to stop. One can regulate its intensity and duration'.[3]

It will be well to quote one case of Forel's at length: 'A thoroughly respectable servant girl suffered in the summer of 1888 from profuse menstruation, which increased in spite of medicines, until in the autumn the periods set in every fortnight, and lasted for a whole week. The girl, who had always been pale, became extremely anaemic, and looked as pale as a ghost. She lost her appetite, and slept very badly,

tration and intensity of mind, our present-day experience and observation will not permit us to assert the improbability of His perception in this case   (Cf Emile Boirac, *The Psychology of the Future*, pp. 175-231.)

[1] 'And the woman, knowing what had happened to her, came forward in fear and trembling and fell down before him, telling him all the truth' (Moffatt).

[2] *Les Guérisons miraculeuses modernes*, p. 17.

[3] *Hypnotism*, trans. by H. W. Armit, p. 110.

mostly only dozing during the night, and experiencing bad dreams. Her master, whom I knew personally, told me of this sad condition, and himself thought that she would have to return to her parents in the country, and that she would probably not recover. I requested him to bring the girl to me. It was evening, and she had been losing excessively, as usual, for four days. I told her to sit down in an armchair and to look at me. She had scarcely fixed her eyes on my finger when her lids closed. I then suggested catalepsy, anaesthesia, &c., with good result. This encouraged me to suggest an immediate cessation of the menstruation. This suggestion was given in connexion with touching of the abdomen, and declaring that the blood flowed into the arms and the legs from the pelvis, and it succeeded in a few minutes. Finally, I suggested good sleep and a good appetite. I gave orders in her home that the housekeeper was to control her menstruation. The loss did not recur, and the girl slept fairly well during the following night. I hypnotized her again a few times, and ordered the next menstruation to appear four weeks later, to be sparse, and to last for two and a half days only. I obtained a good deep sleep in the course of three or four days, and a reasonable appetite after a week, by means of suggestion. . . . The next menstruation arrived after twenty-seven days (one day too soon) at the hour suggested, was sparse, and only lasted for two days. Since then the girl has menstruated regularly every four weeks; the loss remained moderate in quantity, and did not last for more than three days (in response to my suggestion). Her colour returned after a few weeks, and since then she has been able to carry out her duties regularly without interruption, although she is still somewhat weak and anaemic. She has not been hypnotized again, save once, on which occasion she had again become somewhat exhausted and had lost her appetite (April, 1889). She was still quite well in 1895, but I have not seen her since.'[1]

[1] Op cit., p. 249 f For further examples see p. 256 f. On p. 111 Forel refers to the work of Delius who records 60 cases of menstrual disturbances which were nearly all cured by suggestion, or very materially improved (see Delius, ' The Influence of Cerebral Processes on Menstruation and the Treatment of Disturbances of Menstruation by Hypnotic Suggestion ' [*Wiener Klinische Rundschau*, Nos. 11 and 12, 1905]).

XIII

WOMAN WITH A 'SPIRIT OF INFIRMITY'

Lk. xiii. 10-17.

THIS story falls in a section (Lk. xiii. 1-17) peculiar to Lk.
The preceding half of the section contains the passage about
Pilate mingling the blood of the Galileans with their sacrifices, and the parable about the man who had a fig-tree
which bore no fruit. The whole section is sandwiched
between passages which are held by many scholars to belong
to Q.[1].

Since we have no means of knowing what Lk.'s 'source'
for the story was we must remain in doubt as to the value of
the evidence.

> Ἦν δὲ διδάσκων ἐν μιᾷ τῶν συναγωγῶν ἐν τοῖς σάββασιν. καὶ
> ἰδοὺ γυνὴ πνεῦμα ἔχουσα ἀσθενείας ἔτη δέκα ὀκτώ, καὶ ἦν συν-
> κύπτουσα καὶ μὴ δυναμένη ἀνακύψαι εἰς τὸ παντελές.

The scene is laid indefinitely 'in one of the synagogues'.
The interest of the story for the writer lies (as is so often to
be observed) not in the miracle, but in the controversy about
the Sabbath. We have here another example of disease
being attributed to demonic influence by Lk.[2] It is possible
that the phrase πνεῦμα ἀσθενείας is an inference from the words
put into the mouth of Jesus in ver. 16: ταύτην . . . ἣν ἔδησεν ὁ
Σατανᾶς κ. τ. λ.[3]

The cure: Jesus noticed the woman, and called to her,
Woman, you are released from your infirmity (γύναι, ἀπολέ-
λυσαι ἀπὸ τῆς ἀσθενείας σου). He laid His hands on her, and
instantly she became erect (ἀνωρθώθη) and glorified God.

It is not possible to make a diagnosis of the disease with
any confidence. It is, however, open to us to suggest that
the case may have been similar to that of a young sailor

---

[1] E.g., Holtzmann, Harnack. See Moffatt, *I.L.N.T.*, p. 200.
[2] Cf. Lk. iv. 39.
[3] See above, p. 115.

cured by Dr. Pierre Janet 'παραχρῆμα' under hypnosis. I give the case in Dr. Janet's own words: 'Un jeune marin de 19 ans, atteint d'hystéro-épilepsie et anesthésique de presque tout le corps reçoit un choc assez violent au bas de la poitrine. Il n'eut en réalité aucun mal, mais il resta complètement courbé en avant dans la position la plus pénible, qu'il gardait depuis un mois, quand M. le Dr. Pillet, médecin-major de l'hôpital, m'offrit obligeamment de l'examiner. Tous les muscles antérieurs de la poitrine et de l'abdomen étaient contracturés et il était impossible de le redresser. Ce fut cette fois par l'hypnotisme que je cherchai à atteindre l'idée fixe qui évidemment tenait sous sa dépendance cette contracture vraiment systématique. Je l'endors très facilement et, sans rien lui commander, je lui demande simplement s'il peut se redresser. "Pourquoi pas?" répondit-il de ce ton bête qu'ont les somnambules au début du sommeil. — "Eh! bien, alors, redresse-toi, mon garçon." C'est ce qu'il fit immédiatement et l'on put constater que la guérison se maintint très bien après le réveil.'[1]

XIV

DROPSY

Lk. xiv. 1–6.

THE story is peculiar to Lk. It follows a passage from Q (the lament over Jerusalem, Lk. xiii. 34, 35 = Mt. xxiii. 37-9). In this instance again the account is focussed on the Sabbath controversy. The scene is laid in the house of a ruler who was a Pharisee; the day is the Sabbath. Apart from the fact that the incident did not take place in a synagogue there is a striking resemblance between the conditions here and those recorded in the case of the man with the withered hand (Mk. iii. 1–6, &c.) and that of the infirm woman (Lk. xiii. 11–17). Αὐτοὶ ἦσαν παρατηρούμενοι αὐτόν reminds us of Mk. iii. 2 (καὶ παρετήρουν αὐτόν) and the Lucan parallel (vi. 7), in which

---

[1] ' *L'Automatisme psychologique*,' 8ᵐᵉ éd., p. 361.

latter it is expressly said that it was the Scribes and Pharisees who watched him closely. In all these three cases Jesus is described as performing the cure unasked and seemingly in order to drive home His teaching. (On this point see above, p. 93)

In the present case the only indication we have of the malady from which the patient suffered is that he is described as ὑδρωπικός. We are told that Jesus took hold of the man and cured him, and sent him away¹ (καὶ ἐπιλαβόμενος ἰάσατο αὐτὸν καὶ ἀπέλυσεν).

Dropsy (a term not commonly used in medical language at the present day) is generally a symptom of an organic disease—usually disease of the heart or of the kidneys. It is nevertheless open to those who wish to believe that the symptoms in the present instance were not organic in origin to claim that a man described as ὑδρωπικός may be held with some justification to have been suffering from an 'hysterical' affection. There are, indeed, few (if any) diseases which may not be simulated 'hysterically'.²

Physicians occasionally encounter a malady of 'nervous' origin which manifests itself in oedema or swelling of various parts of the body, and which, at any rate to the layman, exhibits the clinical picture of 'dropsy'. A doctor informs me of a case of this kind which came under his care while he was House Physician at Guy's Hospital. The patient was an officer in the army. Suddenly without any warning a part of his body (e.g. the abdomen) would swell up to an excessive degree, and then, after a short period (perhaps an hour), the swelling would subside again. The affliction necessitated the unfortunate man's keeping three different sizes in hats (the symptom sometimes appearing in the head).

¹ If, as seems probable, this is the correct interpretation of ἀπολύειν here, it suggests that the patient had come in order to be cured.
² On the question of the mental healing of 'dropsy' cf. Baudouin, cited above, p. 12, n. 2. There is a disease known as Angio Neurotic Oedema which I understand to be a functional complaint. It is possible that a man suffering from this would be termed ὑδρωπικός.

XV

RESTORATION OF EAR OF HIGH PRIEST'S SERVANT

Lk. xxii. 47–53; [Mk. xiv. 43–52; Mt. xxvi. 47–56; Jn. xviii. 1–11].

ALL the four Evangelists record the striking off of the ear of the High Priest's servant (Jn. gives the man's name as Malchus). Lk. alone says that Jesus healed him.

Verses 49–51 : 49 ἰδόντες δὲ οἱ περὶ αὐτὸν τὸ ἐσόμενον εἶπαν Κύριε, εἰ πατάξομεν ἐν μαχαίρῃ; 50 καὶ ἐπάταξεν εἷς τις ἐξ αὐτῶν τοῦ ἀρχιερέως τὸν δοῦλον καὶ ἀφεῖλεν τὸ οὖς αὐτοῦ τὸ δεξιόν.[1] 51 ἀποκριθεὶς[2] δὲ ὁ Ἰησοῦς εἶπεν Ἔατε ἕως τούτου· καὶ ἁψάμενος τοῦ ὠτίου ἰάσατο αὐτόν.

For those who are disinclined to accept a miracle of healing which seems to run contrary to all the facts of experience this is a particularly difficult one to accept. The instantaneous restoration of a severed limb, they would say, is without even the most remote analogy. If we wish to do so it is not difficult here to modify or explain away Lk.'s version of the incident. The silence of all the other Gospels about the cure rightly makes us very chary of believing in the likelihood of Lk.'s account · without knowing the source from which he obtained his information—and unfortunately there is no probability that we shall ever learn this. But it is well to remember that honest recollections of such an exciting scene as that with which we are concerned are likely to present different, and even conflicting, pictures. Indeed, it is a safe generalization to say that the greater the number of eye-witnesses of the event whose reminiscences come down to us the more conflicting will be our information concerning that event. A scrutiny of Lk.'s version will, I think, lead to the conclusion that he is utilizing at least two sources, and that

[1] One is inevitably suspicious of this detail in Lk. Cf Lk. vi. 6.
[2] ? referring back to the deliberative question εἰ πατάξομεν κ.τ.λ. (49).

the evidence of these two sources conflicts. In ver. 50 he
follows Mk. in saying that the man's ear was cut off; but the
statement in ver. 51 that 'touching the ear' Jesus healed him
is inconsistent with this   Ver. 51 by itself clearly suggests
that the ear was not completely severed.   Moreover, ver. 50
(Marcan source) follows the question εἰ πατάξομεν ἐν μαχαίρῃ in
ver. 49 (non-Marcan) most clumsily, while ver. 51, beginning
with ἀποκριθείς, fits equally clumsily to the preceding ver. 50
It therefore looks as though Lk. had conflated two traditions;
(1) that of Mk., which simply records that the man's ear was
cut off, and (2) a tradition which tells of the healing of the
ear which had been wounded by a stroke with a sword.[1]

XVI

RAISINGS FROM THE DEAD

IN the Synoptics and Acts in addition to the Johannine
story of Lazarus already referred to it is recorded of four
different people that they were restored to life after actual
death (at any rate this is obviously the impression which the
writers of the narratives as we have them intend to convey).[2]
I do not propose in this essay to deal with these cases in
detail, and this not because I think that the stories should be
rejected out of hand, but because of the impossibility of
ascertaining whether death really had occurred.   If the
restored folk had actually died no parallel can be adduced
from modern scientific medical practice, for in the eyes of
a twentieth-century practitioner a person who has been
'restored to life' *eo ipso* can never have died, and, however
assured prior to the re-animation a doctor may have been

---

[1] There is a variant reading in ver. 51. in D a e ff[2] r for καὶ ἁψάμενος . . .
αὐτόν is found καὶ ἐκτείνας τὴν χεῖρα ἥψατο αὐτοῦ καὶ ἀπεκατεστάθη τὸ οὖς
αὐτοῦ.   It has been suggested that the account of the cure is due to a misunderstanding of an Aramaic original which really referred to the restoring (or
the command to restore) the sword to its sheath.

[2] This essay is not concerned with the narratives of the Resurrection of our
Lord.

that death had taken place, after that re animation he would indubitably claim that he had been mistaken in his previous diagnosis.

As regards the N.T. cases with which we are concerned, it is open to any one who admits their general historical accuracy to hold that they provide us with examples of so-called 'suspended animation'. On this assumption modern parallels can, of course, be cited.[1] I have not felt, however, that any useful purpose would be achieved here by quoting at length such instances.

The four cases in the Synoptics and Acts are : —

(1) Jairus's daughter (Mk. v. 21-4, 35-43 ; Lk. viii. 40-2, 49-56 ; Mt. ix. 18-19, 23-6). It must suffice to say that the evidence for this story is probably as good and convincing as that of any narrative in the Synoptic Gospels.

(2) The Nain widow's son (Lk. vii. 11-17). We must remain in doubt as to the value of this narrative peculiar to Lk. It is likely that it was introduced intentionally just prior to the reply (ver. 22) to the Baptist's inquiry (but this does not necessarily invalidate its historicity). It is possible that the account has been influenced by 1 Kings xvii. 17-24, and 2 Kings iv. 33-7. As has been pointed out, Shunem is within half an hour of Nain.[2] Note, there is no mention of 'faith' on the part of any of the dramatis personae. Lk. is rather suspiciously fond of 'only-' children (cf. viii. 42, ix. 38).

(3) Raising of Tabitha by Peter at Joppa (Acts ix. 36 ff.). This belongs to the 'Judean section' of Acts. There is an obvious similarity between Peter's words and behaviour and those of our Lord in the account of Jairus's daughter. But, after all, is not that what might have been expected if Peter was present at the raising of the latter (see Mk. v. 37)?

(4) Eutychus (Acts xx. 9 f.). This incident occurs in a 'we-passage' and therefore the evidence for it is of a high order. The question is are we to lay stress on the words ἤρθη νεκρός[3] or on Paul's statement ἡ ψυχὴ αὐτοῦ ἐν αὐτῷ ἐστίν ?[4]

---

[1] Cf , e.g. the cases cited by Mr. J. M. Thompson, *M N. T.*, p. 44 ; also those reported by T. J. Hudson, *The Law of Psychic Phenomena*, 7th ed., p. 310 ff., and p. 354.

[2] See Dr. A. J. Grieve, *P.C.*, p. 730.

[3] He was taken up dead.

[4] His life is in him.

XVII

GENERAL SUMMARY AND CONCLUSION

THE examination of data undertaken in this essay exhibits the fact that we cannot show with certainty that any given case in the N.T. has its parallel in the annals of modern healing by psychotherapy. This is not because the indications respecting diseases provided by the N.T. writers point in all, or even in most, cases to complaints that are not amenable to mental treatment, but because these indications are, as a rule, extremely vague and do not admit of the possibility of making a sure diagnosis of the maladies in question. In the majority of instances the details supplied suggest a number of alternative disabilities to which they would be applicable. For some of these alternatives it would be difficult and perhaps impossible to find modern parallels where the cure has been brought about by means similar to those apparently employed in the examples under consideration. On the other hand the particulars of the miracles of healing upon which most reliance can be placed are not themselves incompatible with the view that such healing was accomplished through the agency of ascertainable psychological laws.

The absence of sufficient details to allow of a tolerably confident diagnosis is especially to be observed in the cases of 'leprosy', 'fever', 'paralysis' (including 'withered hand'), 'lameness', 'blindness' (excluding that of Paul), 'spirit of infirmity', and 'dropsy'. We approach nearer to certainty, I think, in the case of the 'deaf stammerer', and that of the woman with a haemorrhage. If the argument in this essay respecting the nature of 'demon possession' is sound, here too we may make a diagnosis with reasonable confidence.[1] It should be noted that, in the N.T., cases of this type are treated as though the patient actually is possessed by a demon or demons. Thus a method was employed which

[1] An exception should be made in the case of the Syrophoenician's daughter where no definite symptoms are indicated.

differs from that which is used at the present time in treating cases of what I have taken to be a similar kind. This points to a difference in the healer's theory and underlying belief, which, however, affects the method of cure only superficially. Fundamentally, no doubt, the ancient method is the same as the modern, viz. 'suggestion'. It makes little difference for therapeutic purposes whether the patient believes that the demon has left him or that 'he never has been 'possessed' but has been the victim of morbid mental processes, so long as he is persuaded and has accepted the 'suggestion' that he is free from his slavery.[1]

The Synoptists record two instances of our Lord's healing 'at a distance': the Syrophoenician's daughter (Mk. vii. 24–30; Mt. xv. 21–8), and the Centurion's servant (Mt. viii. 5–13; Lk. vii. 1–10).[2] Even if we could tell what was the matter with these patients there would be no chance of being able to adduce parallels from modern 'orthodox' psychotherapy, because, at least in practice, it does not take into account the possibility of 'distant' healing. The experience of men and women who spend time in prayer for the sick would lead one to suspect that scientific psychologists have still something to learn in this matter.[3]

There is one feature in the cures described in the N.T. which distinguishes them from the majority of modern cures by psychotherapy, and that is the speed with which they were accomplished.[4] No doubt the brief accounts of the Evangelists sometimes mislead us into supposing that the cures were more rapid than they actually were, but at any rate we have no good grounds for believing that any of the patients about whom the narratives tell us needed more than one 'treatment' to be healed. It is open to us to argue, if we wish, that these more frequent speedy cures were due partly to the greater 'credulity' of folk at that period, and partly to the personality of the physician, but that they were

[1] It should be observed, however, that the cure is likely to be more permanent in the second case than in the first. A demon that has departed may possibly come back again—a feat not possible to one which does not exist. (Cf. Mt xii. 43–5 = Lk. xi. 24–6.)
[2] Cf. Jn. iv. 46–54. See above, p 26
[3] The success of 'absent treatment' is in the nature of the case one of the most difficult things to prove.
[4] But cf. above, p. 8.

I 2

dependent upon the same laws which are operative in bringing about healing by modern psychotherapy.

It is necessary to be clear that the belief that Jesus worked His cures in accordance with universal natural laws does not inevitably imply the further belief that His healing was merely healing by 'suggestion'. Were this the case we should be forced to conclude that the large majority of His cures were probably only temporary. For present-day evidence goes to show that treatment by 'suggestion' alone (whether hypnotic or otherwise) leads as a rule to much less permanent results than other forms of psychotherapy.[1] I do not think that it is simply prejudice which causes the Christian to reject the view that our Lord's healing was in the main of a superficial and temporary character. We are not furnished with the subsequent histories of any of His patients which would enable us to base an argument one way or the other on the ground of such direct evidence.[2] On the other hand, if we take the slight indications provided of His method of healing together with His teaching about God, we shall, I think, be led to the conclusion that it was not His practice merely to 'suggest away' symptoms, but that He restored the whole personality of the sufferer, placing him in a new and right relation to life as a whole. 'The important thing for Christ', writes the late Mr. A. C. Turner, 'was not the bodily healing, but the spiritual healing and the faith which both made the bodily healing possible and gave it its saving grace. It is very good that psychical cures should be understood and practised intelligently; but the important thing for *faith*-healing remains the spiritual change—a new belief and confidence in the power and reality of the love of God—on which it lays its chief emphasis.'[3]

The word 'faith' is the key by which we may gain insight into the necessary conditions for healing of the kind performed by our Lord and His followers. The teaching of Jesus leaves us in no doubt about this.[4] What, then, is the meaning of πίστις and its cognates in the N.T.?

---

[1] The effects of suggestion in hypnosis appear to be the least lasting of all.
[2] Is the case of Mary Magdalene an exception to this statement? See Lk. viii. 2.
[3] *Concerning Prayer* (a volume of Essays by a group of writers), p. 403.
[4] Cf. the effect of unbelief at Nazareth, Mk. vi. 1-6 = Mt. xiii. 53-8.

These words (as is not surprising) are employed to indicate various shades of meaning; and yet, at least in the four Gospels and in the writings of the Apostle Paul, there is one outstanding and primary sense which they bear, and that is 'trust', 'confidence'. This 'confidence' is not the result of mere uncritical 'suggestibility'—proneness to accept external suggestions forcibly conveyed. It is confidence in a person; and the person is 'God', 'the Father'—a name to which Jesus gave a wealth of meaning hitherto undreamed of; a meaning which included the attributes of sovereign power and unlimited love. The Father, the Source from which Jesus drew His strength, has the affection for His children and ability to succour them of the best of earthly fathers raised to an infinite degree. εἰ οὖν ὑμεῖς πονηροὶ ὄντες οἴδατε δόματα ἀγαθὰ διδόναι τοῖς τέκνοις ὑμῶν, πόσῳ μᾶλλον ὁ πατὴρ ὑμῶν ὁ ἐν τοῖς οὐρανοῖς δώσει ἀγαθὰ τοῖς αἰτοῦσιν αὐτόν.[1]

In order to illustrate the meaning of the word 'faith' I cannot do better than quote from an admirable discussion of the subject by Mr. C. H. Dodd in his book *The Meaning of Paul for To-day* :—'In the theological constructions which have been based upon Paul the term "faith" has suffered such twistings and turnings that it has almost lost definition of meaning. Indeed, even in Paul's own use of the word there is very great complexity. Perhaps, however, we may get a clue from his use of the familiar words "faith to remove mountains". The expression echoes a saying of Jesus Christ; and we shall not go far wrong in starting from the use Jesus made of the word. "Have faith in God" was the one condition He propounded to those who sought His help.[2] By that is clearly meant trust, confidence directed towards God as the Father and Friend of men. This is the meaning of the word to Paul.[3] As it is Christ who not only shows us the God in whom we trust, but who has also Himself cleared away obstacles and made such trust possible, faith is alternatively described as "the faith of Christ", or

---

[1] 'If ye then, being evil, know how to give good gifts unto your children, how much more shall your Father which is in heaven give good things to them that ask him?', Mt. vii. 11; cf. Lk. xi. 13

[2] 1 Cor. xiii. 2, cf. Mk. xi. 22-3.

[3] 1 Thess. i. 8.

"faith towards Christ".[1] That, however, is for Paul in no way different from faith in God. God is in the last resort the object of faith, for "God is trustworthy" [πιστὸς ὁ θεός]. That is the fundamental postulate of Paul's belief: God is worthy of our trust.[2] It remains for us to trust Him sufficiently to let Him act.'[3]

It may be thought that there is insufficient evidence to show the probability that the N.T. healings were at any rate for the most part of a radical, and not merely superficial, character. I question whether such a position is a sound one. We need constantly to remind ourselves of the 'scrappiness' of our records. Owing to this lack of detail we are wise if we take well into account casual remarks in the narratives which may at first sight appear to have little bearing on the main theme.

Now there are such incidental notices in many of the healing stories which at the very least hint that that 'faith' which Jesus undoubtedly taught to be imperative if a cure was to be wrought was ultimately a confidence in God, and involved a living relationship with God.[4] It is true that the patients seem to have been cured of their symptoms by a trust in the healer and a belief in his ability to heal them without any thought of God's activity in the matter. But there are clear indications that in some cases (and we may justly infer in more cases than those in which such indications are given) Jesus, after the cure, taught them that God was the all-important factor in their well-being, just as, according to Acts, Peter insists that it is not he or the other Apostles who do the healing, but Jesus Christ (cf. Acts iii. 12, 16, iv. 10, 12, ix. 34). For example, after the Gerasene demoniac had been cured he wanted to follow Jesus, but Jesus would

---

[1] Rom. iii. 22, 26, Gal ii 16, iii. 22, Eph. iii. 12, Phil. iii. 9 ('the genitive is *not* subjective in any case'); Col. ii. 5. 'Πίστις ἐν Χριστῷ is probably not exactly what we mean by "faith in Christ" · it is rather faith towards God as conditioned by communion with Christ, Col. i. 4, Eph. i. 15.'

[2] 1 Cor. i 9, x. 13, 2 Cor. i. 18, 1 Thess v. 24.

[3] *The Meaning of Paul for To-Day*, by Prof. C. H Dodd, p. 107.

[4] Πάντα δυνατὰ τῷ πιστεύοντι (Mk. ix. 23, cf. xi. 22). That which avails for healing avails to bring a patient into a new life in every regard According to Jn. ὁ πιστεύων εἰς τὸν υἱὸν ἔχει ζωὴν αἰώνιον (iii. 36). This involves much more than a healing of symptoms : nothing less than a healing and heightening

not allow him to do so, but told him to go to his own home and people and tell them what God had done to him.[1] Again, in the case of the Capernaum paralytic, Jesus, by pronouncing the forgiveness of the man's sins, employed a method other than that of simply suggesting away symptoms, and one which involved a radical change in the patient's relationship with God. But further, the Gospel narrative leaves us in no doubt that there was a fundamental connexion between the healing powers of Jesus and His own prayer-life. Thus He explains the failure of the disciples in dealing with the 'epileptic' boy by saying, τοῦτο τὸ γένος ἐν οὐδενὶ δύναται ἐξελθεῖν εἰ μὴ ἐν προσευχῇ[2] (Mk. ix. 29; cf. Mt. xvii. 20). Compare this with Mk. i. 35 which describes Him going to a desert place to pray, after a day spent in healing.[3] Do we not also read of His praying when, in His treating the 'deaf stammerer', we read that ἀναβλέψας εἰς τὸν οὐρανὸν ἐστέναξεν?[4] This prayer-activity seems to have been essential to the success of the healing ministry, and this fact may dispose us to believe that our Lord by His communion with God was mediating Divine power to His patients. Whatever may be our theory about them, the facts themselves show us that there was an element in Christ's way of healing which is but rarely, if ever, an accompaniment of treatment by 'suggestion' as it is commonly practised at the present day. That teaching of the Fourth Gospel which is subsumed under the words ἐγὼ ἦλθον ἵνα ζωὴν ἔχωσι καὶ περισσὸν ἔχωσιν[5] is an accurate expression in the language of purpose of that which was witnessed of the daily life of our Lord on earth according to the Synoptic Gospels. Jesus cured by bringing to the sufferers life, and His contact with them, whether physical or psychical, was a life-giving contact; that is to say He brought them into touch with God. Whether or not this communion with the Divine was always conscious our

---

[1] Mk. (v. 19) says, ὅσα ὁ κύριός σοι πεποίηκεν. ὁ κύριος clearly means here 'God'. If there should be any doubt about this it is dispelled by Lk. (viii. 39) who says, ὅσα σοι ἐποίησεν ὁ θεός.

[2] 'This kind can come out by nothing, save by prayer.'

[3] This prayer, indeed, came after the healing; but was not the need for it a need for recuperation? N.B. According to Jn. Jesus prayed before the raising of Lazarus (see Jn. xi. 41, 42).

[4] 'Looking up to heaven he groaned', Mk. vii. 34   Cf. Rom. viii. 26.

[5] 'I came that they may have life, and may have it abundantly', Jn. x. 10.

narratives do not tell us, but there is evidence that in some cases our Lord made clear to the patients the source of their well-being, and it seems consonant with His character to conjecture that He did this invariably.

If the argument in the discussion above is valid it follows that modern scientific psychotherapy, while it may (and, I think, does) very considerably help our understanding of the cures in the N.T., yet does not supply us with a complete explanation of them. To take this view is not necessarily to attribute these cures to miracle, if by 'miracle' we mean a transaction which does not in all respects comply with natural laws. It is rather, I should say, to maintain, what no true scientist would dispute, that there are laws of the Universe which are still waiting to be discovered by painful research. Those who believe in a God who is good without qualification must *eo ipso* believe in a God who is consistent without qualification; and consistency involves 'law' as postulated in natural science. This being so, when science turns its attentions to religion it may in time be able to formulate new laws which will manifest just as constant a validity as any that are now admitted in the physical sphere. It is no part of this essay to investigate the matter, but I venture to suggest that if we are truly to understand the miracles of healing in the N.T. we shall have to discover the secret already at least partially revealed to those who, either singly or in groups, make prayer the chief factor in their healing ministries.

In conclusion it should be observed that the performance of the most amazing marvels is not to be compared spiritually and morally with the act of one who, in a land where ritual uncleanness was held the direst of crimes, voluntarily touches a 'leper' and speaks with kindness in the presence of a crowd to an 'unclean' woman who publicly confesses to have touched him.

ὁ ἑωρακὼς ἐμὲ ἑώρακε τὸν πατέρα

INDEX OF NAMES

Abbott, Dr. E. A., 27, 61, 81.
Abrahams, Dr. Israel, 31, 32, 34 ff.,
    44.
Actuarius, 44.
Adler, Dr. Alfred, 14.
Aegineta, 44.
Aetius, 44.
Alexander, Dr Menzies, 36, 53, 58,
    73
Aretaeus, 55, 58.
Azam, 80.

Bacher, W., 36.
Bacon, Prof. B. W., 86.
Banks, John, 97 f.
Bartlet, Dr. J. Vernon, 60.
Baudouin, Prof. Charles, 8, 10, 11 f.,
    20, 21 f., 49, 120, 126.
Baur, Dr F. C., 107.
Bennett, Dr. W. H , 36.
Berguer, Dr. Georges, 23, 56.
Bernheim, 10.
Bjerre, Dr. Poul, 15, 16, 19, 20, 22,
    120.
Bleuler, Prof , 88.
Boirac, Émile, 72 f., 122
Bonjour, Dr. J., 7, 12, 48 f., 114, 122.
Bousset, 37.
Breasted, J. H., 103.
Briand, Dr. Marcel, 12.
Budge, Dr. E. A. Wallis, 39.
Burkitt, Prof. F. C., 48, 86, 92, 93,
    114, 121.

Cable, Miss Mildred, 61, 64, 67, 69 ff.
Cadbury, Prof. H. J., 25.
Cadman, W. H., 86.
Charcot, 109

Charles, Dr. R. H., 35, 52.
Conybeare, Dr. F. C., 35, 41, 52, 103.
Coué, Émile, 10, 20
Crawley, A. E , 104, 115.
Creighton, Dr. C., 43.

Dalman, Prof. G., 46, 56, 86, 90, 106.
Deissmann, Prof. Adolf, 115
Déjerine, 7.
Delitzsch, F., 42.
Delius, 123.
Dodd, Prof. C. H., 133 f.
Dougall, Miss Lily, 72 f., 93.
Dubois, Dr. Paul, 7, 84, 90 f , 120.
Duhm, B., 32.

Eder, Dr. M. D., 22, 91, 116, 117,
    118 f.
Elmore, W. T, 37, 56, 61, 62, 64

Flournoy, Prof , 77 f., 79.
Forel, Dr. August, 12, 122 f
Fox, George, 97 f.
Franks, Dr. R. S., 37.
Frazer, Sir J. G., 56.
Freud, Prof. Sigmund, 14, 16, 17, 22.

Galen, 55, 58, 81, 103.
Gill, Dr. A. Wilson, 110 ff., 119 f.
Gillet, 14.
Gordon, Dr. R. G., 15, 18, 58.
Grasset, Prof., 90.
Gray, Dr. G. Buchanan, 32, 38, 105.
Grieve, Dr. A. J., 129.

Hadfield, Dr. J. A., 7 ff., 12 ff., 19 f.,
    22, 49, 84, 91.

Harnack, Prof. A , 30, 40, 42, 62, 124.
Harris, Dr. Rendel, 27.
Hart, Dr. Bernard, 15, 19.
Hartenberg, Dr. Paul, 88
Hatch, Dr. Edwin, 46, 107.
Hawkins, Rev. Sir John, 52, 101.
Headlam, Prof. A. C., 42, 90.
Hillel, 35 f.
Hilton, Dr. John, 13.
Hinde, S. L. and H , 104.
Hippocrates, 24, 55, 83.
Hobart, Dr. W K., 24, 53, 55, 81, 83, 92.
Hodgson, Dr. Richard, 80.
Holtzmann, O., 124.
Huck, A., 51.
Hudson, T. J., 72, 129.
Hurst, Dr. A. F., 96 f., 108, 110 ff., 116.
Hyslop, Prof. J. H., 79.

Jackson, Dr. Foakes, 36, 52, 86, 90, 93, 106.
James, Prof. William, 80.
Janet, Dr. Pierre, 60, 64, 73 f., 74 f., 76, 79, 125.
Jones, E H., 71.
Jordan, Prof W. G., 32.
Josephus, 35, 38 f., 57.
Jung, Dr. C. G., 14, 16, 58 f., 76 f., 79, 108.

Kennedy, Prof. A. R. S., 37 f., 43, 44, 45
Kennedy, Prof. H. A. A., 56, 108.

Lagrange, 59, 115.
Lake, Prof. Kirsopp, 52, 86, 90, 93, 106.
Langlois and Seignobos, 107.
Latham and Torrens, 44, 95.
Liébeault, 10, 20.
Loewe, Herbert, 34, 54.
Loisy, Alfred, 42, 50, 56, 81, 86, 102, 114, 115.

McComb, Worcester, and Coriat, 21.

McDougall, Prof William, 15
Menzies, Prof. Allan, 60, 85.
Mesmer, Dr F. A., 7.
Micklem, Rev. N., 56, 89
Moffatt, Prof James, 29, 41, 46, 48, 53, 85, 87, 122, 124.
Moll, Albert, 110.
Montefiore, C. G., 32 ff, 42, 55.
Moore, Prof G. F , 25
Moulton, Dr. J. Hope, 55.
Moulton and Milligan, 105.
Munch, 45.

Nevius, J. L , 61, 62, 63, 65 ff
Nicoll, Dr Maurice, 16 f

Origen, 61.
Osler, Sir William, 43 f., 45.

Peake, Dr. A. S., 32.
Petronius Arbiter, 102 f.
Pfister, Oskar, 7, 91, 108, 120.
Philostratus, 39
Podmore, Frank, 72, 74, 77 f.
Prideaux, Dr. E , 15, 17 ff.
Prince, Dr Morton, 78 ff

Ramsay, Sir William, 83 f.
Ripman, Dr. C H , 108.
Ryle, Dr. R. J., 90, 94 f., 109

Schamberg, Dr. J. F., 43, 44, 45.
Schechter, Dr. S., 31, 32
Schmiedel, Prof. P. W., 30.
Skinner, Prof. John, 36, 38
Smith, Prof. W. Robertson, 37, 44
Souter, Prof. Alexander, 53, 54, 83.
Steffens, 59.
Streeter, Canon B. H , 48.
Suetonius, 102.

Tacitus, 102.
Taylor, Dr. Charles, 35.
Tertullian, 105.
Thompson, Rev. J. M., 29, 30, 47, 48, 53, 81, 129.
Thompson, R. Campbell, 39, 55, 56, 57, 103.

Thomson, J , 104.
Torrey, Prof. C. C., 29, 100.
Trotter, W., 15.
Turner, A. C., 132.

Venables, Dr. J. F., 116 ff.
Vespasian, 38, 102.

Waldstein, A. S., 44.
Warneck, Joh., 56, 61, 62, 63 ff., 68, 103.

Weiss, Dr. B., 87.
Wellhausen, Dr J., 56, 87
Wetterstrand, Dr. Otto Georg, 12, 20, 95, 120.
Wood, H. G., 40, 41, 46, 88.
Wright, Dr. A., 54, 87.

Young, Dr. James, 16 f.

Zeller, Dr. E., 107.

INDEX OF BIBLICAL REFERENCES

The abbreviation ' prls ' attached to references in Mk. indicates that there are corresponding passages in the other Synoptic Gospels. It has been employed only where the full references are unimportant.

		PAGE
GENESIS		
xxxii. 29	. . . .	56
EXODUS		
xv. 26 .	. .	31
xxxiv. 30	. . .	59
LEVITICUS		
xiii. f. .	. . .	43
xiii. 46	. . .	47
xiii. 47–59 .	. .	45
xiv. 33–53 .	. .	45
xv. 25, 27	. .	121
xvii. 7 .	. . .	37
xxvi .	. .	31
DEUTERONOMY		
xxviii. 15 ff. .	. .	31
JUDGES		
ix. 23 .	.	36
1 SAMUEL		
x. 5 .	. . .	63
xvi. 14–23 .	. .	36
xviii. 10	. . .	36
xix. 9 .	. .	36
1 KINGS		
xvii. 17–24 .	. .	129
xxii. 19–23 .	. .	36
2 KINGS		
iii. 15, 16 a .	. . .	63
iv 33–7	. . . .	129
v .	. . . .	48
xxiii. 8 b	. . . .	38

		PAGE
JOB		
i. 6 ff. .	. . . .	36 f
v. 17 .	. . . .	32
PSALMS		
vi .	. . .	31
xxxii .	. . .	31
xxxvii .	. . . .	32
xxxviii .	. . . .	31
xlix .	. . . .	32
li .	. . . .	31
lxxiii .	. . . .	32
cii .	. . . .	31
PROVERBS		
iii. 11, 12	. .	32
ISAIAH		
xiii. 21	. . .	37
xix 14 .	. . .	37
xxxiv. 14	. . .	38
xxxv. 6	. 99, 100, 115
lxv. 4 .	. . .	54
ZECHARIAH		
iii 1, 2	. . . .	37
MATTHEW		
vii. 11 .	.	133
vii. 22 .	.	61
viii. 1–4	.	45 ff
vii. 5–13	. 26, 131
viii. 13	. . .	57
vii. 14–15	. .	81 f.
viii. 16	.	47
viii. 28–34 .	.	53 ff.
viii 29	. .	52

MATTHEW (cont.)   PAGE

	PAGE
ix. 1–8	85 ff.
ix. 18–19, 23–6	129
ix. 20–22	120 ff.
ix. 22	57
ix. 27	57
ix. 32–4	40
ix. 32, 33	115 f.
x. 8	48
xi. 5	48, 99
xii. 9–14	91 ff.
xii. 13	57
xii. 22–4	40
xii. 28	40 f.
xii. 43–5	131
xiii. 53–8	132
xiv. 13–14	19
xiv. 34–6	19
xv. 21–8	57 f., 131
xv. 29–31	19, 101
xvii. 14–21	58 ff.
xvii. 18	57
xvii. 20	135
xx. 29–34	105
xx. 30	54, 57
xx. 31	57
xxi. 9	57
xxi. 14	99
xxi. 15	57
xviii. 37–9	125
xxvi. 47–56	127

MARK

i. 21–34 prls.	51, 82, 83
i. 23–8	51 ff.
i. 25	24
i. 26	57
i. 29–31	81 f., 104
i. 30	24, 99
i. 31	24, 45, 60
i. 32	47
i. 34	73
i. 35–9 prls.	19
i. 35	60, 135
i. 38	46
i. 39	41
i. 40–5	45 ff.
i. 44 prls.	48
ii. 1–iii. 6	85
ii. 1–12	32 f., 85 ff., 92

MARK (con.)   PAGE

	PAGE
iii. 1–6	91 ff., 125
iii. 7–11 prls.	19
iii. 11	73
iii. 14, 15	41
v. 1–20	53 ff.
v. 19	135
v. 21–24, 35–43	129
v. 23	45
v. 25–34 prls.	102, 120 ff.
v. 41	45, 60, 115
v. 42	60, 121
vi. 1–6	132
vi. 7 prls.	41
vi 12 prls.	41
vi 53–6	19
vii. 24–30	57 f., 131
vii. 31–7	101, 114 ff.
vii. 33	45
vii 34	135
viii. 11, 12	25
viii. 22–6	27, 45, 54, 101 ff.
viii. 23	105
ix. 14–29	58 ff.
ix. 23	134
ix. 25	24
ix 26	57
ix. 27	45
ix. 29	135
ix. 38–41	61
x. 46–52	105 f.
xi. 22–3	133
xi. 22	134
xii. 36	51
xiv. 43–52	127 f.
xvi. 17	61

LUKE

i. 35	52
iv. 27	48
iv. 33–7	51 ff.
iv. 38	24, 81 f., 83
iv. 39	24, 81 f., 124
iv. 40	47
v. 12–16	45 ff.
v. 15, 16	52
v. 17–26	85 ff.
vi. 6–11	91 ff.
vi. 6	127
vi. 7	125 f.

PAGE

LUKE (*cont.*)

		PAGE
vii. 1–10	. . .	26, 131
vii. 11–17	. . .	129
vii. 22	. . .	48, 99
viii. 2	. . .	132
viii. 26–39	. . .	53 ff.
viii. 39	. . .	135
viii. 40–2, 49–56	. . .	129
viii. 43–8	. . .	120 ff.
ix. 10–11	. . .	19
ix. 37–43 a	. . .	58 ff.
ix. 38	. . .	129
ix. 49–50	. . .	61
ix 52	. . .	47
x. 17–24	. . .	40
x. 17	. . .	61
x 33	. . .	47
xi 13	. . .	133
xi. 14–16	. . .	40
xi. 20	. . .	40 f.
xi. 24–6	. . .	131
xiii. 1–17	. . .	124
xiii. 1–5	. . .	33 f.
xiii. 10–17	. . .	40, 124 f.
xiii. 16	. . .	115
xiii. 34–35	. . .	125
xiv. 1–6	. . .	125 f.
xvii. 11–19	. . .	47 f.
xviii. 35–43	. . .	105 f.
xxii. 47–53	. . .	127 f.

JOHN

ii. 20	. . .	52
iii. 36	. . .	134
iv. 46–54	. . .	26 f., 131
iv. 50	. . .	26
v	. . .	27
v. 14	. . .	33 f.
vi. 69	. . .	52
ix	. . .	27
ix. 2	. . .	33
x. 10	. . .	135
xi. 1–44 ff.	. .	27 f
xi. 4	. . .	33 f.
xi. 41–42	. . .	135
xii 31	. . .	41
xiv. 30	. . .	41
xvi. 11	. . .	41
xviii. 1–11	. . .	127

PAGE

ACTS

		PAGE
i.–xv. 35	.	29 f.
iii. 1–iv. 22	.	99 f.
iii 6	. . .	98
iii. 12	. . .	134
iii. 14	. . .	52
iii. 16	. . .	134
iv. 10, 12	. .	134
viii		47
ix. 1–19	. .	106 ff.
ix. 32–5	. .	98
ix. 34	. .	100, 134
ix. 36 ff.	.	129
xiii. 6–12	.	110
xiv. 8 ff.	.	100 f.
xv. 36–xxviii. 31	.	29 f.
xvi. 16–18	.	30, 60 f
xix 13–16	. .	61
xix. 13	. .	35
xx. 9 ff.	.	30, 129
xxi 8	. .	47
xxii. 4–16	.	106 ff.
xxiii 8	.	35
xxvi 9–20	.	106 ff
xxviii. 1–10	.	83
xxviii. 7, 8	.	83 f

ROMANS

iii. 22, 26	. .	134
viii 26	. .	135
xvi 10	. .	40

1 CORINTHIANS

i. 9	. . .	134
v 3–5	. . .	98
v. 5	. . .	40
vii. 5	. . .	40
ix. 1	. . .	106
x. 13	. . .	134
xii–xiv	. . .	108
xiii. 2	. . .	133
xiv. 1–19	. . .	108
xv. 5–8	. . .	106

2 CORINTHIANS

i. 18	. . .	134
ii. 11	. . .	40
x. 10, 11	. . .	108
xi. 14	. . .	40
xii 1–12	. .	108

	PAGE			PAGE
GALATIANS		**1 THESSALONIANS**		
i. 15, 16	106	i. 8	133
ii. 16	134	ii. 18	40
iii. 22	134	v. 24	134
iv. 13, 14	108		
		JAMES	
EPHESIANS		v. 13–16	105
i. 15	134		
iii. 12	134	**1 PETER**	
vi. 11	40	v. 8	40
PHILIPPIANS		**1 JOHN**	
iii. 9	134	iii. 8	40
COLOSSIANS		**REVELATION**	
i. 4	134	iii. 7	52
ii. 5	134		

BIBLIOLIFE

Old Books Deserve a New Life
www.bibliolife.com

Did you know that you can get most of our titles in our trademark **EasyScript**™
print format? **EasyScript**™ provides readers with a larger than average
typeface, for a reading experience that's easier on the eyes.

Did you know that we have an ever-growing collection of books in
many languages?

Order online:
www.bibliolife.com/store

Or to exclusively browse our **EasyScript**™ collection:
www.bibliogrande.com

At BiblioLife, we aim to make knowledge more accessible by
making thousands of titles available to you – quickly and affordably.

Contact us:
BiblioLife
PO Box 21206
Charleston, SC 29413

CPSIA information can be obtained at www.ICGtesting.com
Printed in the USA
LVOW072021261012

304631LV00021B/288/P